ENCYCLOPAEDIA OF EMINENT THINKERS

VOLUME-III: **RABINDRANATH TAGORE**

Encyclopaedia of Eminent Thinkers Series

Vol. I. The Political Thought of **Mahatma Gandhi**
Vol. II. The Political Thought of **Nehru**
Vol. III. The Political Thought of **Rabindra Nath Tagore**
Vol. IV. The Political Thought of **Radhakrishnan**
Vol. V. The Political Thought of **Vinoba**
Vol. VI. The Political Thought of **Aurobindo**
Vol. VII. The Political Thought of **Jayaprakash Narayan**
Vol. VIII. The Political Thought of **Vivekananda**
Vol. IX. The Political Thought of **Ambedkar**
Vol. X. The Political Thought of **M.N. Roy**

About the Author

K.S. Bharathi did his Master's Degree in Gandhian Thought, Peace-Science, Economics, and Political Science. He also did Postgraduate Diplomas in Politics, Public Administration, Population Dynamics, Gandhian Thought, Tourism, and Telgu. He has contributed some articles in learned journals. He is the author of : *Foundation of Gandhian Thought, Gandhi and Humanity, Socio-Religious Thoughts of Mahatma Gandhi, The Philosophy of Sarvodya, The Satyagraha of Mahatma Gandhi, Gandhi and Nehru, Foundations of Ambedkar Thought, The Social Philosophy of Mahatma Gandhi, Gandhian Approach to Rural Development, The Relevance of Gandhi, Gandhi and Vinoba, The Philosophical Foundations of Gandhian Thought, The Political Thought of Gandhi, The Economic Thought of Gandhi, The Social Thought of Gandhi,* and *The Quintessence and Chronology of Gandhi*. At present, he is the Head of the Postgraduate Department of Gandhian Thought of Nagpur University. He is the Chairman of the Board of Studies of Gandhian Thought, member of the Academic Council, member of the Faculty of Social Sciences, member of the Board of Examination, and member of the Doctoral Research Committee of Nagpur University.

ENCYCLOPAEDIA OF EMINENT THINKERS

VOLUME-THREE

THE POLITICAL THOUGHT OF RABINDRANATH TAGORE

K.S. BHARATHI
Head, P.G. Department. of Gandhian Thought
Nagpur University, Nagpur

CONCEPT PUBLISHING COMPANY, NEW DELHI-110 059

ISBN 81-7022-687-2 (Vol. 3)

ISBN 81-7022-684-8 (Series)

First Published 1998

Published and Printed by
Ashok Kumar Mittal
Concept Publishing Company
A/15-16, Commercial Block, Mohan Garden,
NEW DELHI-110059 (India)

Ph 5648039, 5649024
Fax 091-11-5648068

TO
SREENIVASAN

PREFACE

Rabindranath Tagore was not a professional politician but the sufferings of the Indian people moved him to political action and utterance at every critical stage of the National struggle. He became the bard and spokesman of the *Swadeshi* movement in 1906. In 1919, it was again he who first raised the voice of protest against the atrocities at Jalianwalabagh. He wanted Indian political action to be based on a positive programme of national regeneration rather than a blind reaction against foreign rule.

Tagore's political views were a natural growth out of his religious and social ideals. With his faith in the freedom and equality of the individual, it was inevitable that he should be a democrat in his social, economic and political outlook. In the political field, it was his conviction that there should be no discrimination based on religion, language or sex. In his basic political outlook, he was completely at one with the great tradition of liberalism which holds that the government is best which governs the least. He believed in a federal union of smaller autonomous units, for he held that they offered the individual the greatest opportunity of freedom and self-expression.

The life-sketch and sources of influences has been discussed in the first chapter. Religion and politics has been discussed in the second chapter. Hindu-Muslim unity and education has been analysed in the third chapter. *Charkha*, Non-cooperation movement, and Chronology of events have been covered in the fourth, fifth and sixth chapter respectively.

I would like to place on record my indebtedness to scholars and thinkers whose ideas enabled me to bring out this book. I gratefully acknowledge the scholars from whose works I have drawn citations viz. Dr. B.R. Bali, Dr. Ahluwalia, Dr. S.R. Chowdhary, Dr. Sankar Ghose, Dr. Humayun Kabir, and Dr. Rabindranath Tagore.

So far as the writing of this book is concerned, whatever success I have achieved is due to relentless efforts and encouragement of Dr. P.S.G. Kumar, Head, Department of Library and Information Science, Nagpur University. I sincerely express my gratitude to him.

I express my sincere thanks to Mr. S.T. Patale, P.G. Department of Gandhian Thought, Nagpur University, for supplying me a number of books for reference.

I am indebted to Concept Publishing Company, New Delhi for publishing this book in such a short span of time. Finally I hold myself to blame for the errors and shortcomings, if any. This work would not have been completed without the grace of Lord Venkateswara of Tirumala and Alamelu Thayar of Tiruchanur.

K.S. BHARATHI

CONTENTS

Preface 7

1. Life-Sketch and Sources of Influences 11
2. On Religion and Politics 18
3. On Hindu-Muslim Unity and Education 36
4. On *Charkha* 45
5. On Non-Cooperation Movement 63
6. Chronology of Events 87

Bibliography 103

Index 105

1

LIFE-SKETCH AND SOURCES OF INFLUENCES

Tagore was one of the greatest patriots that India produced in the nineteenth century. His love for his motherland was real and pure. He said, "I shall be born in India again and again, with all her poverty, misery and wretchedness I love India best".[1] He brought fresh approach to the problem of India's freedom from the British rule. He led the constructive phase of India's national struggle. Although politically detached, he always protested against injustice as a matter of moral duty. He led an agitation against the partition of Bengal and surrendered his knighthood when he heard of the brutal killings at Jalianwala Bagh in Amritsar. His special emphasis was a rational and humanitarian approach to all national problems.

Born and brought up as an aristocrat and a lover of beauty, he became conscious of his higher mission of bringing man close to each other. In the fulfilment of his mission, he made a unique contribution during this century. He explored political, social and religious areas of human relationship. His philosophy of man is largely based on perception. When he was born, three distinct movements had met in the life of his country. The first was the religio-intellectual movement led by Rammohun Roy which restored confidence in Indians about their religion and culture. The second was the literary movement whose greatest representative was Bankim Chandra Chatterjee. The third was the national movement for the political, economic and social relief of the country.

Tagore was born on 7th August, 1861, in Bengal. He belonged to an eminent and influential Brahmin family of Bengal. By temperament he was artistic, literary. To him, art became the focal point of all existence. Through art and literature he found the importance of wisdom. His grandfather, Raja Dwarakanath was a man of progressive views who helped Rajaram Mohan Roy in his campaign against the practice of *Sati*. His father, Debendranath, was a remarkable and deeply religious man. Rabindranath Tagore was the fourteenth child to his parents.

Tagore was admitted to Oriental Seminary. After coming back from the school he used to play the teacher with the wooden balusters of the railings of the verandah for pupils. He did not stay long in this school and was soon admitted to Normal School. He did not like his class-fellows, who were naughty and nasty. His third brother was very keen on imparting knowledge to him. Early in the morning he had to get up to learn wrestling. After this, he would learn anatomy. At seven, the Mathematics tutor would come. After this, Sitanath Dutt would teach him science. Then came the grammar teacher. In the evening gymnastics master would teach him gymnastics. Then came the drawing teacher and the English teacher.

Tagore was admitted to the Bengal Academy. He made a few friends at this school. When he was eleven years and nine months old, his father came from the Himalayas to invest Tagore with the sacred thread. The *Maharishi* had selected some verses from the *Upanishads* for the occasion. After achieving full Brahminhood, he began to chant *Gayatri* with great enthusiasm. It was difficult for him to understand its meaning. He found great strength and joy in reciting it. His father called him to the Himalayas. Their first halt was at Shantiniketan. Then they went to Amritsar. Then they proceeded to Dalhousie in the Himalayas. His father taught him Sanskrit, English and Astronomy. This tour brought Tagore very close to his father.

Tagore was admitted in St. Xavier School. He did not concentrate much on his studies. He left the school at his fourteenth year. But he did not give up reading. He devoted all his time to read as many books and magazines. Great scholars would visit his home to discuss with his father the scriptures and the sciences. His elder brother, composed new tunes and left it to him to put words into them. Without his help, he might not have developed into the great song writer that he became.

Two private teachers were employed to teach Tagore. The Bengali tutor, Gyan Babu would read two scenes of Macbeth and would lock him in his room till he had rendered those two scenes into Bengali verse. His mother passed away when he was fourteen. His sister-in-law, Kadambari, showered great affection on him. He read out a poem at the Hindu *Mela*. This poem was published in the *Amrita Bazar Patrika*. Soon after his story entitled *Banaphul* published in *Gyanankur*. He wrote a series of lyrics.

Tagore had become a prolific writer. His writings were being published regularly in *Bharati*. His elder brother, Satyendranath Tagore, was the first Indian to become an I.C.S. He accompanied his brother to Ahmedabad where he was working as a judge. His brother had a well equipped library and he used every moment studying those books and also writing for *Bharati*. He was sent to Bombay to stay with a family friend.

Tagore sailed for England on 20th September, 1878. He was admitted to public school at Brighton. He liked the school. Soon he was sent to London. He joined London University and learned English literature and language. He also joined a music school in London. He had not forgotten *Bharati* and was regularly contributing for it. In 1880, he returned to India without any academic qualification. He wrote his first musical drama (*Valmiki Pratibha*). It was staged in the house at Jorasanko and he himself played the role of Valmiki. The play was a great success. He was invited by the Bethune Society to give a lecture on 'Music and Mood'.

An attempt was made to have Tagore go to England to complete his studies. He was afraid of his father and went to Mussoorie. From Mussoorie, he went to Chandranagore. He wrote his first full-length novel, *The Young Queens Market*. After few months, he returned to Calcutta and stayed with his family.

Tagore was married to Mrinalini Devi on 9 December, 1883. He wrote a historical novel, *Mukut for Balak*, and a children's novel, *Rajrishi*. He also wrote several plays during this period. In 1890, he went to England once again but returned to India after two months. In 1898, he was sent to supervise the family estate at Shelaidah on the bank of the Ganges. This gave him an opportunity to know and understand the villagers, to study their customs and traditions and to appreciate their wants and limitations. He wrote many short stories. He had been thinking of starting a school on unconventional lines. The school was started on 22 December, 1901 with five pupils at Santiniketan. The school was called *Brahmacharya Ashrama*. The students were taught gardening, painting, music, dance, drama and games.

Tagore's wife, Mrinalini Devi, passed away on 23 November, 1902. In 1903, his daughter developed symptoms of consumption and died. In 1904, he lost his son. He was greatly upset. He closed the school and went to Shelaidah but came back after six months. In 1907, his youngest son passed away due to cholera. It was during this period that he wrote the famous hymn *Jana Gana Mana* which is our national anthem.

In 1905, when Bengal was partitioned, Tagore inaugurated the *Raksha Bandan* Festival to demonstrate the unity of Bengal. He appealed the people to donate for the National Fund. He also delivered a speech on Boycott in the session of Indian National Congress. In 1912, he was ill. He left for England on 27 May, 1912, arriving in London on 16 June. During his voyage he translated some of his poems and songs into English. The India Society of London brought out the English edition of *Gitanjali* on 1, November. He returned to India on 4 October, 1913. He had been awarded the Nobel Prize. He was also awarded the degree of D.Litt. by the Calcutta University.

Tagore was a poet of human joys and sorrows. His poetry may be considered as a human document. Not only poetry but he made music and art his instruments for communicating his thought to others. These branches of human thought and experience cherish in them a profound faith in man and in the unity of his being with all existence. He never tried to run away from the world of sense-experience. He believed that the world offers an opportunity to man to develop his personality. All problems of life are human problems and are open to human solution. His emphasis was that all the abundance and beauty of things in this world were for man's enjoyment provided he did not lose faith in himself.

Tagore was essentially a poet and an artist and not a philosopher. Still it is possible for us to gather his philosophical ideas from his writings. Through his writings he tried to establish the true relationship of art and life. His attitude towards life and its problems was that of a realist and humanist. His views on social problems of his time were not determined by narrow consideration such as economics, politics and religion but by spiritual vision. To him, social unrest was due to a wrong attitude to life and lack of reverence for the divine in man. The materialistic attitude and too much importance to physical consideration resulted in general discontentment. It is advisable for man to live in the world but be dedicated to the service of his fellow beings by mutual help and to use all resources in making this life worth living.

After 1887 Tagore felt that he could not remain cut off from the life of the nation. Social, political and religious problems attracted the attention of the poet who was confined to the worship of nature and beauty till then. The conditions of his time made his attitude all the more courageous. To him, the root cause of human misery was the narrow, sectarian and selfish approach towards life. Those who are rich merely smile at the poor, without coming forward actively to help the poor.

Tagore never tried to found a system of philosophy, his voluminous writings are an attempt to reconcile metaphysical doctrines of Indian philosophy with the need to respect the dignity of the human individual through love. He said, "When our self is illumined with the light of love, then the negative aspect of its separateness with others loses its finality. When separation was thus overcome, man could see the truth of things in their universality".[2] He condemned the logical attitudes of F.C.S. Schiller on the one hand and naturalism, dogmatism and absolutism on the other. He considered the world as the expression of finite-infinite personality, of man. With his humanist heart he only wished the evolution of a society free from rivalries, greed and hatred.

Tagore will be always remembered as the poet-prophet of integral humanism. After 1930, no voice was raised more loudly and nobly for the freedom of the world than that of Tagore. His sensitive heart always felt the agony at the sight of Indians suffering at the hands of exploiters from within and from without. But he was equally conscious of the broader human interest. To him, freedom of India was connected with the freedom of the whole world.

Tagore was the only person who tried to raise humanity to the level of Ultimate Reality. He did not succeed in what he tried to realise but still refused to lose faith in man. In 1941, he said, "As I look back on the stretch of past years and see crumbling ruins of a proud civilisation lying heaped as a garbage out of history. And yet I shall not commit the grievous sin of losing faith in man accepting his present defeat as final".[3]

Tagore was a great genius who picked up the best from the different thought currents, absorbed many influences indigenous and foreign and integrated them in his personality and achievements in his own way. Under the influence of the liberal tradition of his family and the philosophy of the *Upanishads*, he developed a positive view of life and love of humanity. He carried India's message of love and universal brotherhood to all parts of the world and thus tried to bring East and West together on the pure and lofty platform of human relationship.

Tagore was deeply influenced by the humanist tradition of the Buddha, and the Buddhist way of life appealed to him most. The great compassion which the founder of Buddhism entertained for his fellow beings, his resolve to renounce the world of luxury for relieving mankind from suffering roused Tagore's admiration for Buddhist philosophy. The Lord Buddha suggested freedom of the self from ignorance so that man was relieved of pain. Influenced by this, Tagore stressed that man must come out of the shell of his individual self in order to enter into the larger self of humanity. He said, "To live in perfect goodness is to realise one's life in the infinite. This is the most comprehensive view of life which we can have by our inherent power of the moral vision of the wholeness of life. And the teaching of Buddha is to cultivate this moral power to the highest extent, know that our field of activities is not found to the plane of our narrow self".[4]

Tagore was influenced by the medieval Indian religious and social philosophy. In the spirit of the medieval saints and poets he talked of the divinity of Man. Kabir's direct apprehension of God as the supreme object of love, as a comrade, which finds passionate expression in his poems captivated his imagination and coloured his religious outlook. He translated one hundred poems of Kabir into English.

Early in his youth, Tagore was influenced by humanism of the West, especially love of freedom and the large hearted radicalism of the British people. He accepted the Western definition of humanism that man was the dominant and ultimate reality. He felt that it was only on the basis of humanism that the wide gulf between the East and the West could be bridged, a synthetic culture could be evolved. In his twelve foreign tours, he carried the humanistic message of India and the nationalism of the East for the universal brotherhood, peace and prosperity of all mankind irrespective of nationality, colour and religion.

Tagore was influenced by the Upanisadic principle of the unity of all life. He felt that humanistic and liberal philosophy of India as underlined in the *Upanishads* and *Gita* could help mankind in realising its true aim. He emphasised two points of the ancient Indian philosophy and culture-human solidarity and supremacy of spiritual values. He had no taste for the textual part of the *Upanishads* nor for their ontology and psychology. It was the essential humanism of the *Upanishads* that seemed to have touched him profoundly and helped him to formulate his own religion of Man. He said, "To me the verses of the *Upanishads* and the teaching of Buddha ever have been things of spirit and therefore, endowed with boundless vital growth. I have used them both in my own life and preachings".[5]

Although Tagore's voluminous writings do not contain more than half a dozen references to the *Gita*, he regarded it undoubtedly one of the basic books of Indian life and thought, a most potential and vital source of knowledge and wisdom. In his famous study, *A Vision of Indian History*, he interpreted the war of Kurukshetra as a struggle between two ideals, i.e. the cult of ritualism supported by the Brahmins and the religion of love and freedom of mind as propagated by the Kshatriya clan.

A few weeks before his death Tagore wrote, "I had at one time believed that the springs of civilisation would issue out of the heart of Europe. But today, when I am about to quit the world, the faith has gone bankrupt altogether".[6] He advised all nations to take up the responsibility in future to build a new society devoid of hatred and selfishness. He was of the opinion that only a humanitarian approach could resolve mutual conflict. Dr. S. Radhakrishnan said, "Rabindranath puts forward a plea for mankind by advocating the ideal of a family of nations to which every member will bring his unique gift. This ideal of international unity and national independence will break down barriers of nations and make for sweet harmony".[7]

Tagore breathes his last on 7 August, 1941. He was 80 years and 3 months at the time of his death which took place in his ancestral home in Calcutta. On the death of Tagore on 7 August, Gandhiji wrote, "Gurudev's soul is immortal and he lives though dead. Gurudev longed to serve the world through India and breathed his last while doing so. His experiment is unfinished. His mortal remains are no more but his soul is immortal like ours. Taking in the sense none perishes or dies. None is born. Gurudev lives significantly. His tendencies were universal, mostly heavenly, through which he will be immortal. Shantiniketan, Sriniketan and Visvabharati—all these are manifestations of his action. They were his soul for which Deenabandhu Andrews left this world followed by Gurudev. Our true homage should be the manning of these institutions which he is watching from wherever he may be".

REFERENCES

1. *The Modern Review*, February, 1917.
2. Tagore, *The Religion of Man*, p. 225.
3. Tagore, *Towards Universal Man*, p. 350.
4. Tagore, *Sadhana*, p. 57.
5. *Ibid.*, p. III.
6. Tagore, *Towards Universal Man*, p. 359.
7. S. Radhakrishnan, *Philosophy of Rabindranath Tagore*, p. 285.

2

ON RELIGION AND POLITICS

Tagore recognised the reality of God, Nature and the finite individual, and considered them inseparable. As against the Western attitude to life, Tagore in his number of essays such as *Tapovan, Amar Jagat, Atmabodh* recognised the eternal kinship between human and non-human nature. Man begins his life as a brute which requires the satisfaction of certain physical needs that are immediate. But he can realise the deeper aspect within him. To him, religion consisted in the synthesis and reconciliation of brute nature to what we consider truth in man. He said, "Religion consists in the endeavour of men to cultivate and express those qualities which are inherent in the nature of Man the Eternal, and to have faith in him".[1]

Religion of man consisted in the realisation that man was the ultimate truth and the measure of all things. Tagore did not stop after exalting humanity in comparison with the rest of the universe but also defined Ultimate Reality in terms of human experience. Neither is God transcendent nor man an insignificant creature; both are comrades and participate and contribute towards the running of the universe. Thus he found something common in humanity and divinity. In his religion man is necessary to God as God is necessary to man. He considered man as the maker of reality. He said, "Humanity is necessary factor in the perfecting of the divine truth".[2] The pinnacle of his humanistic interpretation of religion is reached when he said, "My religion is the religion of Man in which the infinite is defined inhumanity".[3] Regarding the nature of God, he said, "Whatever name may have been given to the Divine Reality, it has found its highest place in the history of our religion owing to its human character".[4]

Tagore had an indivisible faith in God and in many of his writings, he has referred to a formless, speechless, colourless, abstract being or God. He said, "A mind all logic is like a knife all blade. It makes the hand bleed that uses it".[5] As to the religion between God and man, he gave humanity a variety of roles. Sometimes man is considered as the art-work of God; sometimes co-worker with God; as friend, a playmate. The aim of describing the various relations between God and man was to exalt humanity's status in the scheme of things. The main idea was to reject abstract notions of Reality and Truth. He did not hesitate to call God as Man-God and Supreme Man. He said, "Our God is also Man. If this is condemned as anthropomorphism, then man should be blamed for being man, and the lover for loving his beloved as a person, and not as a principle of psychology".[6]

Tagore insisted that religion was an attitude of love, love is the highest form of religion. He had no sympathy for metaphysical intuition for it could not connect the final truth with the phenomenal world. To those who denied the reality of the world he would say that once this beautiful world is gone they would be landed in a glorified nothing. Being a human experience religion originated in man's needs, to help one another for achieving perfection. He tried to humanise religion. C.A. Moore said, "Tagore actually finds the ideal of religion in Universal love and service to mankind, in the more humanistic and worldly sense, of service to man as man and in the world".[7] He reminded that only human fellowship could make God real to men.

Tagore explained that the multiplicity and evergrowing richness of the Universe is testimony to the plethoric creativism and love of God. Creation is an expression of God's personality and love. He said, "Love gives evidence to something which is outside us, but which intensely exists and thus stimulates the sense of our own existence".[8] He accepted the philosophy of world-and-life affirmation and believed that love is not an antithesis of, nor external to cognition. It is the symbol of supreme reality and consciousness. Man can realise God only through love. He believed that all sin, evil and vice are due to the defect in the recognition of the mystery of divine love. A false egoism, based on pride, envy, greed and lust for material gain, is the very antithesis of divine love and is the cause of sorrows and sufferings on earth.

Tagore did not believe in the existence of any God, apart from the realities of life and at the same time, he insisted that the realisation of the 'divine' in man should be regarded as the highest ideal of man's life on earth and all his activities should be oriented to that purpose. In *Gitanjali* and in his several other writings, songs and poems, he upholds the glory of the spiritual unity and of man's limitless joy ar happiness in the realisation of the 'Infinite' in him through love. He explained that there is an eternal craving in man for divine perfection and he could attain it only in the realisation of the spiritual unity through love.

It was his sincere conviction that the Hindu religion could stand against the onslaught of Western civilisation, religion and culture on condition that it rose above its dogmatism and superstition. A spiritual religion like that of Tagore which had for its ideal a right heart and a saintly character, which had for its principle love of God and service of man, could make no alliance with useless rites and ceremonies, dogmas and superstitions. He said, "We do not want nowadays temples of worship and outward rites and ceremonies. What we really want is an *ashram*. We want a place where the beauty of nature and the noblest pursuits of man are in sweet harmony. Our temple of worship is there where outward nature and human soul meet in union".[9]

According to Tagore, the religious person must dwell in the world, must work sincerely in making it a fit place for the habitation of God. Worship of God means loyalty and service of the mankind. To those who waste their time, energy and money in the name of religious practices, spend thousands an thousands in building huge temples when the poor starve and die for want of bread, his advice was to serve mankind for being true to God. This idea finds expression in his 'Fruit Gathering', in which a religious man poses to have dedicated everything to the Lord and find himself helpless in offering anything to a poor Brahmin. He said. "Man is true where he feels his infinity, where he is divine. He is unreal when he is surrounded by the walls of ego".[10]

Tagore said, "In any case if there be any truth absolutely unrelated to humanity then for us it is absolutely non-existing".[11] He explained that his religion was rooted in the ideal of the reconciliation of the 'Infinite' or 'God' and the world of nature and man. He addressed his 'God' in the poem as *Jivan Devata*, which is what the name signifies, the God of life. To him, the greatest truth was the revelation of the Infinite Spirit in humanity. There is no contradiction in the simultaneous acceptance of the two aspects of truth—the self-expression of God in multiplicity and the ascension of the finite into the unity and bliss of God. He was not merely the seekers of abstract truth of the philosopher and metaphysician but the truth of life, the truth of day-to-day experience, especially of man's life, its meaning and purpose and fulfilment it may be said that he had laid down the highest standard of honesty and integrity in private, as well as, in public life. His philosophy was nurtured on spiritual foundations inculcating the belief that since man was essentially a spiritual being, he could be best interpreted in the perspective of the eternal and spiritual only.

Tagore explained that he did not want salvation in defying the existing world. He admitted the world of facts and objects but interpreted them finally in terms of the 'Infinite' or in the perspective of spiritual unity, harmony, joy and heavenly bliss. He explained that a really beautiful thing delights us only because we cannot help admitting a truth in it that is ultimate. To him, beauty and truth were identical. He did not belong to the group that is for the dictum 'art for art's sake' or 'beauty for beauty's sake'. Beauty and art, in order to be true, should reflect the truth which is eternal and ultimate. An object of beauty or art remains incomplete if it fails to reflect the highest truth.

Tagore accepted the *Gita*'s ideal of *Karma-Yoga* and asked men to accept the world as a field of spiritual opportunities. Behind his poetic speculation on the relation between man and God was hidden the problem of the relationship between man and society. A feeling of kinship between the individual self and the supreme personality was the philosophical foundation of his lofty humanism.

Tagore explained that the word religion or *dharma* originated from the root 'dhar' or to sustain. A true religion always sustains or nourishes the *sat* or the highest truth in man. He said, "I believe in a spiritual world, not as anything that separates this world, but as the innermost truth. With the breath we draw, we must always feel this truth, that we are living in God".[12] He emphasised that we cannot accept our existence as a momentary outburst of chance drifting on the current of matter towards an eternal nowhere. Life has a purpose to be fulfilled and a true religion helps man to achieve that end. It binds men in a relationship which is beautiful and not merely utilitarian. He said, "When this creative ideal which is dharma gives place to some overmastering passion, then this civilisation bursts into a conflagration like a star that has lighted its own funeral pyre".[13] He explained that in India for people *dharma* has become one with their life. To ask them to sell it, is like asking them to sell their life. They do not claim any personal merit for possessing it.

Tagore identified religion with the highest truths in man's life on earth, which could neither be separated nor viewed independently from man's everyday life and his relationship with others. To him, India has religion which pervades every aspect of man's life. We have no separate religion for the Church, for Sunday, for home and outside as one sees in European countries. In India life and religion are one and the same. A true religion ceased to become a mere dogma or creed but becomes the very essence of life.

Tagore identified Hinduism as an all embracing, living faith, a synthesis of different faiths, customs, traditions and cultures which had been brought by various kinds of people during the different stages of her history. His famous poem *Bharat Thirtha* is based on this ideal. In interpreting India's history, he pointed out that from ancient times, various peoples with widely divergent cultures met on the soil of India. Hence the great problem which India faced from the beginning of her history was how to adjust and harmonise these diverse elements into a happy synthesis. To him, Hinduism being a perpetual process of reconciliation of contradiction, maintains a constant adjustment of opposites in a peaceful harmonious way. He said, "India tolerated difference of races from the first, and that spirit of toleration has acted all through her history. For India has all along been trying experiments in evolving a social unity within which all the different peoples could be held together".[14]

Tagore explained that in India religion has never been treated as only an isolated or private affair. It is regarded as social in character, it covers every aspect of an individual's life, being a giant tree religion in India gives shelter to every one, saves him from the evils of separatism and sectarianism and helps to achieve his mental and moral illumination. He regarded all Indians as Hindus. He said, "India stands before the civilised world as an embodiment of the ideal of 'unity through diversity'. To see the One in the world and within oneself, to instal the One in the midst of the many, to discover it by knowledge, to establish It by action, to realise It in love and to proclaim It in life—this is what India has been doing through the centuries in the face of danger and difficulty and in times of good or bad".[15]

Tagore appealed to Indians to live according to the great spirit of their civilisation and work for the ideal. He dreamt of a day when Hindus, Muslims, Christians and people of different faiths would not fight against each other but would seek and attain a synthesis. He emphasised that this synthesis would not be a un-Hindu but would be peculiarly Hindu. He identified Hindu religion with Indian civilisation and culture as a whole and found therein an unending source of vitality and growth. To him, religion was not a matter of outward observances and formalities but a relentless pursuit after truth, harmony and unity. He said, "There is no religion higher than truth and when religion has to make way for religious organisation, customs, outward observances and others, it is like a river dominated by its sand-bed, the current stagnates and its aspects become desert-like".[16]

Tagore had an immense conviction about the power of the human heart to transcend all limitations those of space and time as well as of caste, race and nationality. His famous Hilbert Lectures in 1930 at Oxford, the Kamala Lectures at Calcutta University in 1933 sounded the grand note of a large humanism. He drew attention to the world of human values and pleaded for a creative approach to life and human relationship.

Tagore was also pained at the division of Hindu society on the basis of caste, religious beliefs and sex. In his view the caste system failed to recognise the flow of life, the inherent oneness of all human beings. It failed to consider that in human beings differences were not like physical barriers. The *Varna* system as it operated amongst the Aryans was a socially uniting force in which different peoples could live together in harmony while having freedom to maintain differences. But the present system has proved to be an instrument of oppression. It must be based on the principle of universal brotherhood and love.

Tagore was also against discrimination on the basis of sex. In all spheres of life he advocated equality for men and women. To him, husband-wife relationship was sacred. That is why in his play *Sati* the character Uma refuses to accept the man as her lover who has not won her affection. He reminded Hindus of their ancient traditions in which a person was looked upon as an individual man or woman and not as a Brahmin, Kshatriya, etc. He felt that unless our old traditions were received there was every possibility of India being isolated and cut off from the current of modern civilisation.

To Tagore, the hierarchy of values incorporated in *Varnashrama* doctrine was right as the scale of values in society depending not upon the amount of wealth but on the development of the soul. He said, "The social organisation of India largely contributed to the freedom from narrowness and intolerance which distinguishes the Hindu religion, a phenomenon which astonished the Europeans who with less jarring elements, have struggled for ages to establish peace and harmony among themselves".[17]

Tagore explained that foreign critics often misread the conservative spirit of India as the trade artifice of an interested priest-craft. He said, "The Brahmins were the guardians of the seed of culture in ancient India and the Kshatriya strove to put into wide use the harvest of wisdom".[18] He insisted that the four divisions system was based on the ideal of unity in diversity, and by prescribing different functions for different groups of people it discouraged artificial competition, mutual jealousy and feeling of disharmony among the people. Though he belonged to the Brahmo Samaj, he had his own peculiar religious ideals. He believed that true *Varnashrama* doctrine was based on the ideals of equality and dignity of labour.

Tagore was of the opinion that it was the sacrifice of the old ideals of *Varnashrama* doctrine in favour of useless rites and observances and resultant growth of a perverted caste that had undermined the liberal spirit of Hinduism making all men *Shudras* at heart. He regretted that the Brahmanas, teachers of the four castes had madly rejected intellect, strayed far from Right Conduct, abandoned their Teacherhood, and became their pupil's pupil.

Tagore explained that he regarded untouchability as an un-Hindu practice. He also explained that inter-caste marriage was known in old Hindu society and could be introduced in near future in Hindu society. This ideal of marriage is in no way un-Hindu but essentially Hindu. He had deep compassion for the untouchables and his criticism of the vice of untouchability has found a living form in his famous poem, 'Oh my unfortunate country' as well as his well known dance drama *Chandalika*. He warned the caste Hindus of the far reaching effects caused by the practice of untouchability. He said, "The dumb fury of the down trodden had created an explosive situation which unless cured by sympathy and love would result in a furious revolution in support of the Universal law of moral balance".[19] He made an appeal to his countrymen to join Gandhiji in his noble task of removing the burden of the ages and to fulfil his vow of fighting to finish the evils of untouchability.

Tagore believed that Hinduism possessed a dynamic vitality to grow, assimilate and change according to the needs of the time and people. He wanted reforms within the traditional Hindu order and appealed to his countrymen to live according to the best teachings of their own religion. He explained that the Brahmo Samaj movement was in no way anti-Hindu in spirit, nor a deviation from the old Hindu ideals, rather it insisted on reform within Hindu fold. He insisted that people did not need to abandon their age old Hinduism but should seek reforms and improvements within its established system and according to the great spirit of their own heritage. He pointed out that the ideal of *Mukti* in Hindu religion was based not on the principle of negation of the existing world but by the affirmation of it through selfless service and disinterested love to others.

To Tagore, truth was the only way to attain spiritual and social fulfilment. He said, "A religion is a knowledge or learning, a science of what is truth".[20] He described 'spiritual freedom' or 'our freedom in truth' the basis of all kinds of social justice. He advocated the purity not only of ends but also of means. His humanism was based on the philosophical acceptance of the Universal eminence of the Super-spirit. He argued that when humanity lacks the music of soul, society becomes a more mechanical arrangement of compartments of political and social classifications for the sake of convenience. He claimed that the spiritual aspect of man was as real as his material counterpart and the later finds its fullest expression only in the perspective of the former.

Full of agony at the blatant exploitation of man in the name of religion, caste and sex, Tagore said, "In the lands where cannibalism is prevalent man looks upon man as his food. In such a country civilisation can never thrive, for there man loses his higher value and is made common indeed".[21] Again he said, "We never can have a true view of man unless we have a love for him. Civilisation must be judged and prized, not by the amount of power it has developed, but by how much it has evolved and given expression to, by its laws and institutions, the love of humanity".[22]

The aim of giving a humanistic interpretation was to help men of all religions and sects in coming closer to one another. Tagore made use of his poetic genius in communicating the highest truth to mankind. His message of love and universal brotherhood will continue to work as a soothing shower over the fire of conflict between men of different beliefs.

Tagore's political views were a natural growth out of his religious and social ideals. With his faith in the freedom and equality of the individual, it was inevitable that he should be a democrat in his social, economic and political outlook. In the political field, it was his conviction that there should be no discrimination based on religion, language or sex. His vision of India was of a federative commonwealth where men and women, speaking different languages, professing different religions, following different customs and pursuing different avocations would have complete equality of opportunity and self-expression. In his basic political outlook, he was completely at one with the great tradition of liberalism which holds that government is best which governs the least.

Tagore's belief in the freedom and dignity of man was derived from his religious faith and reinforced by his acceptance of the humanism which was the prevailing intellectual attitude of his younger days. He accepted without hesitation the western idea of democracy but to this he added the Indian conception of the individual's responsibility for social service. He greatly admired the Indian tradition under which the individual might win wealth and power through political patronage, but could win prestige and honour only from social approbation earned by social service. Freedom and creativity were for him two of the basic values of human life. Perhaps this was derived from his poetic temperament, for there can be no art without free creation. In politics, local autonomy offers the greatest scope for such expression of freedom and creativity of the individual. His aversion against regimentation in any form was thus partly the result of his own temperament and partly due to the impact of western liberal ideas imbibed in his early youth.

Tagore's concern for the individual made him suspicious of large organisation in the economic as well as the political sphere. In politics, he believed in a federal union of smaller autonomous units, for he held that they offered the individual the greatest opportunity of freedom and self-expression. He was anxious to introduce in India the latest techniques of western science while taking steps to retain the freedom and dignity of the individual man and woman. He was throughout his life guided by an integrated outlook that sought to achieve harmony and balance among the different elements that constitute Indian society. The same integral approach led him to combine tradition and experiment in his attempts to solve the problems of human life.

Tagore held that through cooperation, we can also convert our individual weakness into political strength. He held that such cooperation in the political sphere can be best developed through local self-government. The individual finds fulfilment only when he is autonomous. The community flourishes when it is responsible for its own welfare. He believed in decentralisation of authority, for only in this way can human beings establish personal relationship with one another. A large organisation inevitably brings in its wake an element of impersonality, and for him there is no greater menance to human values than such impersonal and abstract relations.

Tagore was one of the earliest among our national leaders to declare that our political subjection was merely an outward expression of inner weakness. The roots of India's bondage lay in her neglect of the individual and her acceptance of a social system which had condemned millions of her children to indignity and humiliation. A merely political programme could not therefore bring about the liberation of India, for such a programme would deal only with the symptoms. He insisted that Indian political activities should not be confined to mere political agitation but find expression through nation building services of various types. He declared that Indians must become self-reliant and develop knowledge, moral purpose and aesthetic perception. Once this development took place, India would forthwith become free. He declared that if we work for economic self-sufficiency and social freedom, political liberty would come automatically.

Tagore extended the principle of the right and dignity of the individual to the case of nations as well. He recognised the right of each nation to work out its own destiny but at the same time he proclaimed that national claims must never encroach upon human obligations. With all his regard for the achievements of western man, he condemned in unqualified terms his political domination and economic exploitation of other regions and peoples. His magnificent hymn to Africa is marked by the deepest human sympathy and is one of the earliest recognition of the rights of the African people to independence and self-realisation in every sphere of life. Love and respect for the ideals of one's own people is a positive virtue, but disrespect for the ideals and traditions of other peoples is a crime against humanity. He was one of the first to see the dangers of the aggressive nationalism which had raised the nation to the status of a demi-God. He proclaimed in unequivocal terms that the blind worship of the Nation State contained the seed of disaster for man. Two World Wars within the space of thirty years have proved how tragically correct his reading was.

Tagore was not a professional politician but the sufferings of the Indian people moved him to political action and utterance at every critical stage of the national struggle. He became the bard and spokesman of the *Swadeshi* movement in 1906. In 1919, it was again he who first raised the voice of protest against the atrocities at Jalianwalabagh. He would not however let his passionate condemnation of the political action of the British Government affect his respect for the British people. He wanted Indian political action to be based on a positive programme of national regeneration rather than a blind reaction against foreign rule. In the days of the *Swadeshi* movement of 1906 and again in the height of the non-cooperation movement in 1920, he did not hesitate to express in the clearest terms his disapproval of certain aspects of the national political programme.

Tagore was a strong believer in the dignity of the individual and the value of freedom and initiative for all nations. It was his passionate belief that India's special contribution to human civilisation lies in her exaltation of the principle of unity in diversity. He believed that differences are in themselves valuable and add to the richness of life. He also believed that there is a divine purpose in the diversity of languages, religions and cultures which are found in Indian life. He proclaimed that the unity of India has been and shall always be a unity in diversity in which every language, every religion and every culture shall have its due place.

Science and Technology have brought into close contact peoples following different economic and political systems. Different religious groups which were formerly geographically separated live today in close proximity and must learn to accommodate one another if the world is not to go up in flames. If these differences are allowed to lead to conflict, the results are bound to be disastrous for all. Tagore taught that these differences should not be suppressed but given their proper place in a larger whole. He pleaded for cooperation and not competition among different ideals. He may said to have laid the foundation of the principle of co-existence of different ideologies which, it is being increasingly recognised, offers today the only hope for the survival of man.

The deep humanism and indeed the religious fervour which coloured his political attitude and belief is best seen in the song he wrote for a session of the Indian National Congress and which has today become the National Anthem. In a sense, it is more a religious hymn for all mankind than a national anthem for any one country. Tagore begins with an invocation to the Lord of the hearts of all the peoples of the world and sings the praise of the eternal charioteer who has guided man through the ups and downs of history. He seeks welfare not for India alone but for the entire world. He sings of endeavour and the cooperative reconstruction of human society in which every individual will be guaranteed the dignity and the rights of a civilised man in a civilised world. The Indian National Anthem, which is one of his greatest gifts to India, thus reflects his ideal of a world where there will be friendship and cooperation among all men and mutual regard and respect among all peoples.[23]

Tagore's political thought centred round his spiritual ideals and religious beliefs which proclaimed clearly, that the highest truth of man's life on earth is self-realisation. He insisted that man's individual, social, economic and political activities should be guided by the supreme ideal of life. He said, "Our fight is a spiritual fight. It is for Man. We are to emancipate Man from the meshes that he himself has woven round him".[24] His political philosophy is proceeded from his deep spiritual humanism. He refused to equate political action with expediency and opportunism; thus he was a great opponent of Machiavellian state-craft in all its forms. He stressed the need for incorporating moral values in politics. He desired to create a spiritual awareness in mundane matters. His creative and cultural significance are thus widely re-emphasised and his meaning is raised to a higher spiritual level. His approach to politics was basically spiritual, having its root deep in his religious conviction that man is essentially a spiritual being.

Tagore believed that human life being an undivided spiritual whole could not be divided into different compartments. He explained that European civilisation was based on the spirit of conflict and separation while Indian civilisation is based on the spirit of unity of the soul. He believed in an immanental cosmic law of moral governance in the world. Any conscious or unconscious violation of the law has to pay its price either by extinction or death. Imperialism, exploitation, despotism, cruelty and other political and social evil thus contain the seeds of self-destruction in themselves. He described law in his Creative Unity as the universal law of moral balance. He believed that the sum total energy of mankind was working towards the fulfilment of the highest spiritual ideal. He believed that all men are marching from epoch to epoch towards the fullest realisation of the soul. He explained that this realisation of soul was greater than the things man accumulated, the deeds he accomplished, the theories he built, the soul whose onward course was never checked by death or destruction. To him, there is no metaphysics in it, the human being is the son of the 'Immortal One', and that 'know—thyself' is the *Summum bonum* of his existence. He said, "I believe that there is an ideal hovering over and permeating the earth, an ideal of that Paradise, which is not the outcome of fancy but the ultimate reality in which all things dwell and move".[25]

Tagore explained that when man looked at the world through the veil of his desires, he made it small and narrow and failed to perceive its full truth. Of course, it is obvious that the world serves him and fulfils his needs, but his relation to the world does not end there. *Ahimsa* becomes an all-pervasive eternal principle applicable to every situation in life without exception. On this basis, any economics or politics, which is based on the spirit of utility only, was unacceptable to him.

He believed that the mental or spiritual was more real than the material. The objective universe is an embodiment of human mind and his love to others.

To Tagore, ends and means were identical terms. Purity of means should be accepted as a comprehensive principle in achieving an end. The separation of politics from moral principles in the name of science or realism was, to him, as a trap to kill the soul. His political ideal was a part of his philosophy of life. He did not make any distinction between an honest ideal and the means of achieving it. He pointed out that success lies more in an honest endeavour than in real fulfilment or accomplishment of that ideal. He said, "Our life is facing the infinite and it is in movement. Its aspiration is, therefore, infinitely more than its achievements".[26] Real life is not that which is being but that which is becoming to him.

In 1941 Tagore gave a message to his countrymen. He said, "As I look around I see the crumbling ruins of a proud civilisation strewn like a vast heap of futility. And yet I shall not commit the grievous sin of losing faith in Man".[27] He explained that man's fight is a spiritual fight, he is always fighting to free himself from the meshes of organisations or systems that he himself has woven round him. To him, in the West 'organisation' is placed before 'man' while in India 'organisation' is placed after 'man'. He was a poet of individuality and not of domination. He championed the cause of individualism against the spirit of organisation in his novels and dramas.

In no way Tagore encouraged unrestricted enjoyment of freedom and rights for the individual. He explained that only in society, man realises his self through a unity with his fellow creatures. This social consciousness or sympathy is the very basis of man's right. He said, "The only true human progress is coincident with the widening of the range of feeling. . . . Man does not acquire rights through occupation of larger space, nor through external conduct, but his rights extend only so far as he is real, and his reality is measured by the scope of his consciousness".[28] He believed that rights in order to be best realised, should proceed from self-imposed responsibilities and duties of the individual towards his fellow beings in society.

Tagore considered intellectual slavery more dangerous than political slavery. He had a spiritual concept of freedom and he did not make any clear-cut distinction between political freedom and spiritual freedom. To him, one was complementary to the other. He said that those who had not achieved *Swaraj* in their inner nature, were deprived of the same in the outside world as well. He added that however determinedly India might try to hunt the monster of foreign dependence with outside lethal weapons it would always elude her pursuit by changing its skin or its colour. But when she would learn to grow from within she could best realise her freedom.

Tagore's poem on Freedom expressed his concept of freedom as it should be. He prayed to God to help him to realise the freedom of the soul which would enable him to stand firm and suffer with strength. He considered suffering based on the strength of the soul to be surest and permanent means of winning *Swaraj*. He explained that India's opportunity for winning freedom would come to her when she could prove that she was morally superior to the people who ruled her by their right of conquest. He said, "She (India) must willingly accept her penance of suffering, the suffering which is the crown of the great. Armed with her utter faith in goodness India should stand unabashed before the arrogance that scoffs at the power of the spirit".[29]

The path of violence, although it seems to be a quick and convenient method, could not bring any permanent and beneficial result. Tagore condemned bitterly the path of violence to be the most ineffective way of winning *Swaraj*. He said, "The way of bloody revolution is not the true way . . . a political revolution is like taking a short-cut to nothing, that the wrong way may appear shorter, but it does not reach the goal and only grievously hurts the feet".[30] He was a great apostle of non-violence. He threw himself actively into the anti-partition movement of Bengal in 1905 but withdrew from the movement in 1906, as terrorism and violence were fast overtaking the anti-partition movement. He stressed the need of constructive and creative nationalism and gave a completely new scheme for the regeneration of Indian society through non-violence and on a constructive or self-help basis, in his articles. It was he who first showed an altogether new way of achieving India's socio-political aspiration in non-violent and constructive way.

Tagore opened a *Swadeshi* store in Calcutta and collected from all parts of the country, various articles of Indian manufacture required for day-to-day living. He stocked everything in the store. He said, "Long before this popular ebullition of excitement I myself had given a thousand rupees, when I had not five rupees to call my own, to open *Swadeshi* store and courted banter and bankruptcy".[31] In the educational field, he was the first person who took the initiative of infusing a spirit of self-help and self-reliance among the people. He established the Santiniketan in 1901. His writings on rural education and on the problem of community development are still the best manual for all works in the field. It was he who took the leading part in establishing the National Council of Education in 1906 and accepted the task of drawing up a comprehensive programme of work for the Council.

While idealising the spirit of self-help and constructive work, Tagore indirectly discouraged self-pity, begging attitude and cowardice among the people. He said, "Weakness is the traitor who betrays our soul".[32] He earnestly desired that the exploited and destitute humanity of India should cultivate moral force for their regeneration and should refuse to bend before the arrogance of despotic violence and the imperialistic might of the West. In 1908, he administered a stern rebuke to the mendicancy of the political leaders of the day and criticised them for the lack of self-confidence in themselves. He declared that he did not belong to the group who believed that running to and fro on king's highroad with petition is the chief work of the country. Thus non-violence to him was not a negative principle but a positive attitude of mind which defies all kinds of sufferings and even death in resisting evil.

Tagore had a grace of combining in him the spirit of nationalism and internationalism. He refused to be drawn into the politics of his times as it was devoid of human feelings. It was politics of narrow nationalism and commercialism. His poems and lectures on 'Nationalism' show that he had a glimpse of the universal. Though he denounced the soulless mechanical trend in European culture, he recognised its contribution in the awakening of India. He had appreciation for the noblest men of modern India like Rammohan Roy who stood alone in his day for India's union with the world on the broad basis of humanity. At the same time he advised not to ape the West but to maintain Indian culture and to feel proud of it.

Tagore emphasised the need of establishing genuine relation between man and man, regardless of nationality. He said, "We must know that every nation is part of humanity and each must answer the questions: what have you to give to man, what new ways have you discovered for his happiness? As soon as a nation loses the vital strength for each discovery, it becomes a dead weight, like a paralysed limb on the body of the universal man".[33] Unless we are prepared to work for a common ideal our national interests cannot be fulfilled. His writings permeate withe the ideal of peace, freedom and universal brotherhood.

Tagore's love for his country was charged with a deep feeling of national pride and honour which refused to bow down to any external threat or coercion or even death. At the same time, it was not based on hatred against any particular country even not against Great Britain. He said, "I love India, not because I cultivate the idolatry of geography, not because I have the chance to be born on her soil but because of the ideal of peace, harmony and universal brotherhood that Indian stood for".[34] He blended patriotism with humanism and did not see any conflict between the two. His patriotism was based on love of mankind. When India suffered from injustice, he stood against it, not as an Indian but as an human being. In 1898, he condemned the policy of lynching of the Negroes in the United States. He felt as much for the Negroes brutally lynched in America as for the Koreans who were the victims of Japanese Imperialism of the time. He was a lover of man, not of any country. To him, India was not merely a geographical expression but was an ideal itself, having its roots in the Vedantic concept of spiritual unity of existence. It is a proclamation of faith in truth, justice and non-violence and the essentially good qualities of man. Indian nationalism is in no way an antithesis to international understanding and peace, rather it is conducive to it, as he interpreted it. He appealed to his countrymen to have faith in their own spiritual mission.

Tagore's nationalism underwent a transformation during his later life under the impact of the excesses of European imperialism. Consequently, he sought the solution of India's political and social problems in the context of international understanding. He thought that unless an ideal type of society was created in India, in which men of different religions and cultures lived in harmony, there was no hope for India. Thus he gave an international outlook to India's nationalism. As for his internationalism, it was a matter of his temperament and an intellectual conviction based on life's experiences. His universalist sympathies came to him from the traditions of his family.

Tagore identified the spirit of Western nationalism with imperialism in general. He wrote that in the West national machinery and commerce and politics compressed bales of humanity which have their use and high market value, but they are bound in iron hoops, labelled and separated off with scientific care and precision. He explained that the word 'Nation' as the people of the West understood it did not exist in India nor occur in our language. Indian history has been the history of continual social adjustment and not that of organised power for defence and aggression as in Europe. He explained that he called India a 'land of the No-Nation' as he did not subscribe to the accepted definition of 'nation' of the West. He interpreted nation in the sense that it was the political and economic union of a people for a mechanical purpose. He said, "If we ever think that to build up the Nation after the European pattern is the only way open and the only way of humanity, we shall be wrong".[35]

Tagore was against Japan's expounded doctrine, 'Asia for the Asiatics'. He did not support Japan's war of aggression on China in the name of 'Asia for Asians'. In 1938 he said, "I have believed in the message of Asia, but I never dreamt that this message could be identified with deeds which brought exhaltation to the heart of Tamer Lame at his terrible efficiency in man slaughter. . . . The doctrine of 'Asia for Asians' which you enunciate in your letter, as an instrument of political blackmail, has all the virtues of lesser Europe which I repudite".[36]

Tagore characterised the European war of Nations as 'the war of retribution'. He said, "The Nation, with all its paraphernalia of power and prosperity, its flags and pious hymns its blasphemous prayers in the Churches and the literary mock thunders of its patriotic bragging, cannot hide the fact that the Nation is the greatest evil for the Nation. Any new birth of its fellow nation in the world is always followed in the mind of other nations, by the dread of new peril".[37] He insisted that isolated independence should not be the goal of the world states. He explained that the spirit of social cooperation or interrelationship should be encouraged in international affairs. Isolated independence of so-called nation—states is a threat to world peace. Every sovereign state with its independent foreign policy and aggressive spirit of nationalism becomes an enemy of other similar nation states. He said, "Civilisation must take its stand upon its basis of social co-operation and not upon that of economic exploitation".[38]

Tagore hoped that international organisation would pave the way of international understanding and peace. He said, "The readjustment of international grievances by mutual agreement of nations is probably one of the best legacies of Geneva".[39] During his visit to Russia, he explained that the strong men of the League of Nations did not really want to stop their far-reaching acts of degradation, however much they may shout for peace. Hence it is that in the imperialist countries the sowing of the thistles of armament outruns the sowing of grain.

Tagore clearly explained that he did not belong to the group who believed that India required to be strong and rich before she could raise her voice for the sake of the whole world. He also explained that the measure of greatness could not be determined by external possession or by material resources. He argued that India in spite of her penury and humiliation, can afford to come to the rescue of humanity. To him, the movement for political independence of India was only a part of a larger task to be accomplished first. The end, to him, was the spiritual liberation of whole mankind.

REFERENCES

1. Tagore, *The Religion of Man*, p. 89.
2. Tagore, *Creative Unity*, p. 80.
3. Tagore, *The Religion of Man*, p. 96.
4. *Ibid.*, p. 205.
5. Tagore, *Stray Birds*, p. 51.
6. Tagore, *The Religion of Man*, p. 114.
7. C.A. Moore, *Tagore—Humanist or Transcendentalist*, p. 228.
8. Tagore, *The Religion of an Artist*, pp. 20-21
9. Tagore, *Sadhana*, p. 41.
10. Tagore, *Personality*, p. 31.
11. Tagore, *The Religion of Man*, p. 223.
12. Selections from the Works of Rabindranath Tagore, p. 20.
13. Tagore, *Lectures and Addresses*, p. 51.
14. *Ibid.*, p. 110.
15. Tagore, *The Message of Indian History*, p. 113.
16. *The Modern Review*, September, 1917.
17. *Ibid.*, December, 1919.
18. Tagore, *A Vision of Indian History*, p. 18.
19. Tagore, *Creative Unity*, p. 127.
20. Tagore, *The Religion of Man*, p. 77.
21. Tagore, *Sadhana*, p. 108.
22. *Ibid.*, p. 111.
23. *Rabindranath Tagore—A Centenary Volume*. pp. 149-52.
24. *Letters to a Friend*, pp. 127-28.
25. Tagore, *The Religion of an Artist*, p. 31.
26. Tagore, *Sadhana*, p. 52.
27. Tagore, *The Religion of Man*, p. 68.
28. Tagore, *Sadhana*, pp. 18-19.
29. *Letter to Gandhi*, 12-4-1919.
30. *The Modern Review*, October, 1921.
31. *Letters to a Friend*, pp. 13-33.
32. Tagore, *Poems*, No. 60.
33. Tagore, *Towards Universal Man*, p. 64.
34. Tagore, *A Vision of Indian History*, p. 45.
35. *Rabindra Rachanavali* Vol. IV, p. 424.
36. Sochin Sen, *The Political Thought of Tagore*, p. 137.
37. *Nationalism*.
38. *Ibid*.
39. R.K. Prabhu and Rao. *The Mind of Mahatma Gandhi*, pp. 159-61.

3

ON HINDU-MUSLIM UNITY AND EDUCATION

A person who is integrated and sure of himself fears none and consequently provokes no fear. To Tagore, salvation from ego or the principle of self-realisation should not be regarded only as an individualistic aim, but as a collective aim. He looked forward to a day when the principle of the identity of selves no longer pertains only to the spiritual experiences of a few but finds its application in collective life as well. The principle of self-realisation denotes the act of moralisation of one's own surroundings also. He regarded the issue concerning Hindu-Muslim unity as an end in itself. The doctrine of the end justifying the means had no appeal to him, He never thought of using the phenomena as an anti-British propaganda used for winning certain political gains.

Tagore wrote that Hindu-Muslim unity was required not only for safeguarding minority interest but for internal growth and enrichment of Indian culture itself, which is a combination of the Hindu and Muslim cultures as a whole. He said, "Muslims had come to India with a culture which was aggressively antagonistic to her own. But in her saints, the spirit of the *Upanishads* worked in order to attain fundamental harmony between the things that were apparently irreconcilable".[1] He always maintained a sympathy and fellow feeling for his Muslim brothers and sisters. In his many short stories, he depicted the Muslim characters with an utmost and amazing sympathy, love and fellow feelings for them. He always defended the cause of the poor Muslim community. He believed that they had always been economically and politically exploited by the so-called clever Hindu leaders of society. He appealed to his Hindu brothers to take the special initiative of dispelling some of the misgivings and distrust that incidentally grew up in the minds of the Muslims during their long association with the Hindus.

Tagore, said, "It is futile to expect a lasting bridge between the two to be made with the feeble cement of brotherhood manufactured on the Congress Platform".[2] He appealed to his countrymen not to make the issue a political game or mix it with the political happenings of the day. Even he was critical of the so-called Hindu's support to the Khilafat cause. He explained that mere political support to the Khilafat movement would not solve the real problem concerning Hindu-Muslim unity.

Tagore maintained that the British rulers in India following their peculiar policy of 'divide and rule' always helped to widen the gap between the two communities. To him, the so-called Hindu-Muslim problem was an artificial growth of the late British period in India. In 1932 he said, "I find from personal observations that this strife (between Hindus and Muslims) has been going on for the past twenty-five years only. Before this period there was, as far as I can recall—and I have lived for many years in the village—no such animosity and enmity between them".[3]

Tagore appealed to the ruling authority not to interfere in the matters related to Hindu-Muslim relationship. The British administrator's involvements in so-called local matters would make things worse and unmanageable. In 1908 he said, "This conflict is bound to die in course of time. Government would hardly be equal to fanning the flame for all time to come. . . . If the houses of subjects are set in flame, some time or other through uncertain directions the fire is likely to spread up to the premises of the king's palace".[4] Mutual tolerance and racial equality should be taken as the fundamental principles, not as a temporary measure of establishing Hindu-Muslim unity. He maintained that real harmony and peace would be possible only when the Hindus and Muslims would be treated on an equal footing. Muslims should be given equal opportunities and privileges in society like that of the Hindus and thus the root cause of fear, distrust and disappointment in the Minds of the Muslims could be eliminated. He appealed to his Hindu friends to extend job opportunities, education privileges, and honourable social and Governmental positions to their Muslim brothers, so that they could psychologically feel more assured and satisfied.

Tagore appealed to both the Hindus and the Muslims to cast off the shackles of or free their minds from the grip of unmeaning and non-essential traditions and customs of their religious and work for real unity. He said, "Religion unfolds the key to salvation whereas the religious system invites the bondage of slavery".[5] He analysed the essential differences between a Hindu and a Muslim. He appealed to both of them to overcome their mutual exclusiveness or hindrances from within. He said, "The country where religion prescribes the hatred of man, where people are doomed to perdition for the drinking of water from the hands of a neighbour. . . . Those who have isolated themselves, those who are overpowered by a spirit of exclusiveness rather than the spirit of oneness, they have no escape from the bondage of poverty, insult and slavery".[6] He emphasised the fact that the British could not be blamed, as the sins of the two communities became the source of their strength; British rule was merely a symptom of the disease. The Hindu-Muslim conflict was deepening because the British were only fomenting the trouble which had already been there.

Tagore made no specific comment on intermarriage among Hindu and Muslims, yet he made it clear that to refuse food served by a Muslim friend on the ground of religion was itself a crime against humanity and God. He was against the elimination of all kinds of religious and social differences between the two communities by coercion or by the logic of expediency. He explained that Hinduism in a real sense asked everybody to follow his own religion in the true sense of the term, and at the same time, not becoming a threat to others in doing the same. Hinduism recognises the differences between communities as real and beneficial to the common good of the society, it seeks to establish 'unity in diversity' or harmony among differences.

Tagore explained that he had full faith in the good sense of Muslims. He did not share the view of those who argued that the Muslims did some acts including cow slaughtering only to provoke the Hindus against them. He explained that the ideal of unity should always be placed before the so-called religion which preached separation and division. He said, "When religion tells me that I should be friendly with the Musalmans, I accept that reverently without a word of argument for the truth underlying the dictum is for me as the great ocean itself. When religious orthodoxy asked him to reject food served by his Muslim friend, they are really placing the priest before deity and thus insulting the religion in whose name they dare to speak".[7]

Tagore was against the so-called 'two nation' theory given by some Muslim politicians of the time and supported by the British rulers. He did not live long enough to see the birth of Pakistan. His views regarding the Partition of Bengal, his active involvement in the anti-Partition drive, his enthusiastic move to start *Rakhi-Bandhan* ceremony, as a symbol of Hindu-Muslim unity clearly show that he was totally against the 'two nation' theory. In 1908 he said, "Muslims are in a majority on the eastern side of Bengal. . . . This Muslim zone is bound up with Hindus on account of uniformity in language, literature and education. If Bengal is divided into two zones, the Muslim zone and the Hindu zone, then all the ties that bind Hindus and Muslims will be unloosened by and by . . . if the king proposes to widen the gulf . . . in course of time Hindu-Muslim exclusiveness and intensity of mutual jealousy will be undoubtedly on the increase. In fine, in this unfortunate country it is not difficult to create disunity, the basic problem is how to achieve unity".[8]

Tagore pointed out that the Muslims might differ from the Hindus in religion and social customs but that did not mean that they constituted a separate nationality. The Muslims constitute an indivisible part of Indian nationality as do the Hindus. He appealed to his countrymen to resist firmly the partition drive enunciated by the British rulers. He said, "We shall remain firm where we have our own strength; we shall remain alive to our duty; we shall place reliance on those who are our own people. We shall not despair, nor shall we complain against the conduct of the Government. . . . We want no favours; governmental hostility will increase our prowess".[9] He could not accept disunity, as the last word on Hindu-Muslim relations.

Tagore's basic apprehension was that the division of the country into different Muslim zones and Hindu zones would complete the phase of disruption, and would be disastrous to the age-old Indian civilisation, based on the spirit of unity in diversity. He stood for the awakening of different sects, different communities. He believed that every particular community had its own distinctive features, special contribution to enrich human civilisation. This consciousness of one's own culture and tradition helps one to rise to greatness. He insisted that unity could come only when the two parties were equally strong and enlightened. The Muslims should be given full opportunities and privileges to develop from within and, then and then only, an effective unity could be attained.

Tagore was a great idealist in educational philosophy as well as experimentalist to the core. He said, "To attain full manhood is the ultimate end of education, everything else is subordinate of it".[10] He explained that unity of truth could be attained only when there is no separation of relationship between the intellectual, physical and spiritual aspects of education but a harmony prevails. He also explained that the highest education is not that which gives one information but sets one's life in harmony with all existence. Mere collection of facts belongs to the outside world while true education is related to the inner soul of things.

To Tagore, the aim of education was individual in the sense that it ensures freedom or salvation of individual soul from all kinds of bondage—superstition, ignorance, egocentric impulses or narrowness of mind. He said, "In the typical thought of India it is held that the true deliverance of man is from ignorance".[11] The process of individual development and social progress are interdependent to such an extent that one is inconceivable apart from the other. The aspiration of man for an everexpanding future has two aspects that are interrelated—One is individual fullness and the other is social fullness. He clearly pointed out that there is no gap between the two. The highest aim of education is to provide or create an ideal atmosphere of knowledge and truth so that the essential individuality of each person may bloom fully in conformity with the highest good of society.

Tagore stood for unlimited freedom in the sphere of education. His approach was negative. He pointed out that it was his quest for freedom from the routine school life in early age, which led him to the establishment of a school in Shantiniketan where children could enjoy maximum freedom of learning with minimum restriction. He condemned the traditional way of teaching in the existing schools of his time. He said, "It is a mere method of discipline which refuses to take into account the individual. It is a manufactory specially designed for grinding out uniform results".[12] In his writings he indicated the need of formulating some elaborate code of good manners for the students. He insisted on the need for introducing India's age-old *Brahmacharya* ideals in his school and advised his student to follow the rules in good spirit and with determination of mind. He said, "It is the purpose of *Brahmacharya* to protect in soothing quiet the budding stage of the human personality from the premature stimulation of instincts and the excitement of luxury".[13]

In upholding the old *ashram* ideals based on a close teacher-students relationship, Tagore said, "In India we still cherish in our memory the tradition of the forest colonies of great teachers. . . . This ideal of education through sharing a life of high aspiration with one's master took possession of my mind".[14] He explained that it was with this ideal in his mind he started his school , where he claimed, his students were fortunate enough to be able to receive their lessons from a living teacher and not from text-books. He insisted that teachers should occupy a pivotal position in Indian's future educational system. Without systematic efforts to improve their quality, it would be impossible to make India's educational institutions more purposeful. It is for the teachers to mould the character of the younger generation which is entrusted to their care, they are in a real sense, the great architects of a nation.

Tagore relied less on bookish knowledge and stressed more on activity centred education. He said, "We have come to this world to accept it, not merely to know it. We may become powerful by knowledge, but we attain fullness by sympathy".[15] He explained that there is an inseparable bond between physical and mental faculties and a child learns more through his senses than by other means. An intelligent use of bodily organs in a child provides the best and quickest way of developing his intellect. He said, "True education is to realise at every step how our training and knowledge have organic connection with our surroundings".[16] He insisted that India's future educational system should be in full touch with her complete life, economical, intellectual, aesthetic, social and spiritual. The educational institutions should be in the very heart of her society, connected with it by the living bonds of varied cooperation.

Tagore arranged the teaching of handicrafts side by side with the so-called liberal education. He agree that a child learns more through his senses and the primary business of a school should be to train children in cooperative and mutually helpful living by providing them maximum opportunity to use muscles, sight, feeling as well as hearing and by employment of energy, originality and initiative. He included 'Art' as an integral part of education of his institution and insisted on permanent cooperation between the artists and craftsmen. The Kala Bhavan in Shantiniketan under constant encouragement and support of Tagore and Abanindranath Tagore developed a new type of decorative art based on Indian tradition but suited to the new ideals of modern life.

Tagore recognised the greatness of all religions and upheld the underlying truths and values of every religion of the world and provided the scope of studying different religions in his institutions. The students of his institution belong to different castes, creeds, religions and provinces and are treated on equal footing. He explained that teaching of religion could never be imparted in the form of lessons, it is there where there is religion in living. He explained that in 'Shantiniketan' he wanted to create an unseen atmosphere of aspiration where children could feel that they are always in communion with God. He said, "I believe in a spiritual world, not as anything separate from the world, but as its innermost truth. With the breath we draw, we must always feel this truth, that we are living in God. The experience of this spiritual world has to be gained by the children by fully living in it and not through the medium of theological instruction".[17]

Tagore believed that society itself is a school and its conscious and unconscious influences mould the mind and character of its people. Hence educational institutions must make arrangements for moulding youth into patterns approved by her society. He believed that the educational system introduced by the British rulers and particularly, the ulterior aim of Lord Macaulay was very contrary to the spiritual heritage, economic interest, cultural integrity of Indian people as a whole. In 1906, he first took an active initiative in establishing a 'National Council of Education' for making arrangements for imparting national education to the youth of India and thereby to save them from the evil effects of the prevailing educational system.

In 1892 Tagore emphasised the need of teaching through one's mother tongue and pointed out the defects of using English as medium of learning. He said, "We study words unaccompanied by any ideas, and when we grow up the exact opposite happens—ideas come to us but we have no words to express them".[18] He insisted that the excessive burden to learn through a foreign medium had sapped the strength, enthusiasm, freshness and vitality of the minds of India's youngmen. He believed in the greatness of English and its literature and recognised its utility as the world language for international business, cultural exchanges and understanding. He would encourage its study among those who had special linguistic talent and interest. He said, "The foreign ship may bring imported goods into a port but she cannot help to distribute them among inland markets".[19]

Tagore believed that as an individual finds his fullest expression being a member of a society, a nation finds its fullest entity only by being a member of an international community. He explained that he had no distrust of any culture because of its foreign character, what he objected to was the artificial arrangement by which foreign education tends to occupy all the space of our national mind, and, thus kills or hampers the great opportunity for the creation of a new thought-power by new combination of truths. He explained that he did not share the view of some people who maintain that Western culture was the only source of knowledge. He said, "The star could give us light but not the day, it may give the direction but can never open the full view of truth before our eyes".[20] He insisted that education should not be dragged out of its native element, the life current of the people. He believed that only in education lies the true path of international understanding and peace.

Tagore glorified simplicity and austerity, the key to educational attainment and success. He said, "Poverty brings us into complete touch with life and the world for living richly is living mostly by proxy, and thus living in a world of lesser reality. This may be good for one's pleasure and pride, but not for one's education".[21] He believed that nature and a rural environment were important agencies. He was not interested in segregating the child from the baneful influence of man and his society. He himself raised and answered the question whether he had attained his ideal in his institution—he explained that the attainment of his deepest ideals, were difficult to measure by outward standards. He accepted man as 'he is' or with all his inequities and incompleteness and tried to improve them. He never lost faith in the good sense of the human mind and believed that it was bound to respond to any act of love, sympathy, truth and justice.

According to Tagore all problems, political, social and economic were due to ignorance and lack of education. Whatever education was available, did not cater to the needs of the society. Instead of arousing the sense of oneness, it only divided the society into artificial and inhuman segments. He said, "The highest education is that which does not merely give us information but makes our life in harmony with all existence".[22] He was of the opinion that education must not aim to fill the brains with knowledge but must also create sympathy in the educated person for all the contemporary practices in education not only ignore this ideal but systematically make persons indifferent and self-centred. A child is forced to undergo a discipline which is imposed on him through unnatural methods.

REFERENCES

1. *Rabindra Rachanavali,* Vol, III, p. 550.
2. *The Modern Review*, January, 1924.
3. Rabindranath Tagore, *Letters from Russia*, p. 179.
4. *Rabindra Rachanavali*, Vol, X. pp. 500-501.
5. *Ibid.*, Vol. XXIV, pp. 353-58.
6. *Ibid.*, Vol. X, pp. 628-29.
7. *The Modern Review*, January, 1924.
8. *Rabindra Rachanavali*, Vol, X, pp. 522-24.
9. *Ibid.*, Vol. X. p. 616.
10. Rabindranath Tagore, *Akanksa Shantiniketan*, *Paus* 1326 B.S.

11. Rabindranath Tagore, *Sadhana*, p. 78.
12. Rabindranath Tagore, *Lectures and Addresses*, pp. 18-19.
13. *Siksa*, 1342, B.S. ed., p. 51.
14. Rabindranath Tagore, *Lectures and Addresses*, pp. 28-29.
15. *Ibid.*, p. 21.
16. Rabindranath Tagore, *The Centre of Indian Culture*, Visva Bharati, p. 2.
17. Rabindranath Tagore, *Lectures and Addresses*, p. 28.
18. *Rabindranath Rachanavali*, Vol. XII, p. 288.
19. *The Modern Review*, October, 1917.
20. Rabindranath Tagore, *An Eastern University*, pp. 73-74.
21. Rabindranath Tagore, *Lectures and Addresses*, p. 25.
22. *Ibid.*, p. 21.

4

ON CHARKHA

Tagore had no zeal for *Khadi* and the *Charkha* and he publicly expressed his opinions against the cult of spinning. Gandhi visited Santiniketan in 1925. Tagore received him with great respect. He could not be convinced that the *Charkha* was or could ever be anything more than one of the many necessary village crafts. He explained his viewpoint in an article 'The Cult of the *Charkha*' in the *Modern Review* of September, 1925.

Acharya Prafulla Chandra Ray has marked me with his censure in printer's ink, for that I have been unable to display enthusiasm in the turning of the *Charkha*. But because it is impossible for him to be pitiless to me, even when awarding punishment, he has provided me with a companion in my ignominy in the illustrious person of Acharya Brajendra Nath Seal. That has taken away the pain of it, and also given me fresh proof of the eternal human truth, that we are in agreement with some people and with some others we are not. It only proves that while creating man's mind, God did not have for his model the spider mentality doomed to a perpetual conformity in its production of web and that it is an outrage upon human nature to force it through a mill and reduce it to some standardised commodity of uniform size and shape and purpose.

When in my younger days I used to go boating on the river, the boatmen of Jagannath Ghat would swarm around, each pressing on me the service of his own particular vessel. My selection once made, however, there would be no further trouble; for, if the boats were many so were the passengers; and the places to go were likewise various. But suppose one of the boats had been specially hall-marked, as the one and only sacred ferry by some dream emanating from the shrine of Tarakeshwar, then indeed it would have been difficult to withstand the extortions of its touts, despite the inner conviction of the travellers that though the shore opposite may be one, its landing places are many and diversely situated.

Our *Shastras* tell us that the divine *shakti* is many-sided, so that a host of different factors operate in the work of creation. In death these merge into sameness; for chaos alone is uniform. God has given to man many-sided *shakti*, for which reason the civilisation of his creation have their divine wealth of diversity. It is God's purpose that in the societies of man the various should be strung together into a garland of unity; while often the mortal providence of our public life, greedy for particular results, seeks to knead them all into a lump of uniformity. That is why we see in the concerns of this world so many identically liveried machine-made workers, so many marionettes pulled by the same string; and on other hand, wherever human spirit has not been reduced to the coldness of collapse, we also see perpetual rebelliousness against this mechanical mortar-pounded homogeneity.

If in any country we find no symptom of such rebellion, if we find its people submissively or contentedly prone on the dust, in dumb terror of some master's bludgeon, or blind acceptance of some *guru's* injunction, then indeed should we known that for such a country, in extremis, it is high time to mourn.

In our country this ominous process of being levelled down into sameness has long been at work. Every individual of every caste has his function assigned to him, together with the obsession into which he has been hypnotized, that, since he is bound by some divine mandate, accepted by his first ancestor, it would be sinful for him to seek relief therefrom. This imitation of the social scheme of anti-life makes very easy the performance of petty routine duties, but specially difficult the attainment of manhood's estate. It imparts skill to the limbs of the man who is a bondsman, whose labour is drudgery; but it kills the mind of a man who is a doer, whose work is creation. So in India, during long ages past, we have the spectacle of only a repetition of that which has gone before.

In the process of this continuous grind India has acquired a distaste for very existence. In dread of the perpetuation of this same grind, through the eternal repetition of birth, she is ready to intern all mental faculties in absolute inaction in order to cut at the root of *Karma* itself. For only too well has she realised, in the dreary round of her daily habit, the terribleness of this everlasting recapitulation. Moreover, this dreariness is not the only loss sustained by those who have suffered themselves to be reduced to a machine-like existence; for they have also lost all power to combat aggression or exploitation. From age to age they have been assaulted by the strong, defrauded by the cunning and deluded by the gurus to whom their conscience was surrendered. Such a state of abject passivity has become easy because of the teaching that through an immutable decree of Providence they have been set adrift on the sea of Time, upon the raft of a monotonous living death, burdened with a vocation that makes no allowance for variation in human nature.

But whatever our *Shastras* may or may not have said, this popular conception of the Creator's doing is the very opposite of what he really did do to man at the moment of his creation. Instead of furnishing him with an automatically revolving grindstone, God slipped into his constitution that most lively sprightly thing called *Mind.* And unless man can be made to get rid of this mind, it will remain impossible to convert him into a machine. Insofar as the man at the top succeeded in paralysing the people's minds by fear, or greed for hypnotic texts, they succeeded in extorting, from one class of them, only textiles from their looms; from another class, only pots from their wheels; from a third, only oil from their mills. Now when from such persons as these, it becomes necessary to demand the application of their mind to any big work on hand, they stand atlast. "Mind!" cry they. "What on earth is that? Why don't you order us what to do and give some text for us to repeat from mouth to mouth and age to age?"

Our mind, in doing duty only as a hedge to prevent the encroachment of living ideas, had been kept evenly clipped short for the purpose. If, in spite of that, in this age of self-assertion, we find mischievous branches trying to make room for the disturbance of the spruceness of the trimming,—if all our minds refuse incessantly to reverberate some one set *mantram*, in the droning chirp of the cicadas of the night,—let no one be annoyed or alarmed; for only because of this does the attainment of *Swaraj* become thinkable!

That is why I am not ashamed, —though there is every reason to be afraid,—to admit that the depths of my mind have not been moved by the *Charkha* agitation. This may be counted by many as sheer presumption on my part. They may even wax abusive; for swearing in a much needed relief for the feelings when even one stray fish happens to elude the all-embracing net. Still I cannot help hoping that there are others who are in the same plight as myself,—though it is difficult to find them all out. For even where hands are reluctant to work the spindle, mouths are all the more busy spinning its praises.

I am strongly of opinion that all intense pressure of persuasion brought upon the crowd psychology is unhealthy for it. Some strong and wide-spread intoxication of belief among a vast number of men can suddenly produce a convenient uniformity of purpose immense and powerful. It seems for the moment a miracle of a wholesale conversion; and a catastrophic phenomenon of this nature stuns our national mind, raising high some hope of easy realisation which is very much like boom in the business market. The amazingly immediate success is no criterion of its reality, the very dimension of its triumph having a dangerous effect of producing sudden and universal eclipse of our judgement. Human nature has its elasticity; and in the name of urgency, it can be forced towards a particular direction far beyond its normal and wholesome limits. But the rebound is sure to follow, and the consequent disillusionment will leave behind it a desert track of demoralisation. We have had our experience of this in the tremendous exultation lately produced by the imaginary easy prospect of Hindu-Muslim unity. And therefore I am afraid of a blind faith on a very large scale in the *Charkha* in the country which is so liable to succumb to the lure of short-cuts when pointed out by a personality about whose moral earnestness they can have no doubt.

Anyhow, what I say is this. If, today, poverty has come upon our country, we should know that the root cause is complexly ramified and it dwells within ourselves. For the whole country to fall upon only one of its external symptoms with the application of one and the same remedy, will not serve to fight the demon away. If man had been a mindless image of stone, a defect in his features might have been cured with hammer and chisel; but when his shrunken features bespeak vital poverty, the cure must be constitutional, not formal; and repeated hammer strokes upon some one particular external point will only damage that same life still more.

In the days when our country had to bear the brunt of Moghul and Pathan, the little jerry-built edifices of Hindu sovereignty fell to pieces on every side. There was then no dearth of home-spun thread, but that did not serve to bind these into stability. And yet, in those days, there was no economic antagonism between the people and their rulers. The throne of the latter was established on the soil of the country, so that the ripe fruits fell to the ground where the trees stood. Can it then be today—when we have not one or two kinds, but a veritable flood of them, sweeping away our life-stuffs across the seas away from our motherland, causing it to lose both its fruits and its fertility,—can it be, I say, that the lack of sufficient thread prevents our stemming this current ? It is not rather our lack of vitality, our lack of union?

Some will urge that though in the days of Moghul and Pathan we had not sovereign power, we had at least a sufficiency of food and clothing. When the river is not flowing, it may be possible to bank up little pools in its bed to hold water enough for our needs, conveniently at hand for each. But can such banks guarding our scanty economic resources for local use withstand the shocks which come upon it today from far and near? No longer will it be possible to hide ourselves away from commerce with the outside world. Moreover such isolation itself would be the greatest of deprivations for us. If, therefore, we cannot rouse the forces of our mind, in adequate strength to take our due part in this traffic of exchanging commodities, our grain will continue to be consumed by others, leaving only the chaff as our own portion. In Bengal we have a nursery rhyme which soothes the infant with the assurance that it will get the lollipop if only it twirls its hands. But it is a likely policy to reassure grown up people by telling them that they will get their *Swaraj* that is to say, get rid of all poverty, in spite of their social habits that are a perpetual impediment and mental habits producing inertia of intellect and will,—by simply twirling away with their hands? No! If we have to get rid of poverty, which is visible outside, it can only be done by rousing our inward forces of wisdom, of fellowship and mutual trust which make for cooperation.

But, it may be argued, does not external work react on the mind? It does, only if it has its constant suggestions to our intellect, which is the master, and not merely its commands for our muscles, which are slaves. In this clerk-mechanical ridden country, for instance, we all know that the routine of clerkship is not mentally stimulating. By doing the same thing day after day, mechanical skill may be acquired; but the mind, like a mill-turning bullock, will be kept going round and round a narrow range of habit. That is why, in every country man has looked down on work which involves this kind of mechanical repetition. Carlyle may have proclaimed the dignity of labour in his stentorian accents, but a still louder cry has gone up from humanity, age after age, testifying to its indignity. 'The wise man sacrifices the half to avert a total loss', so says our Sanskrit proverb. Rather than die of starvation, one can understand a man preferring to allow his mind to be killed. But it would be a cruel joke to try to console him by talking of the dignity of such sacrifice.

In fact, humanity has ever been beset with the grave problem, how to rescue the large majority of the people from being reduced to the stage of machines. It is my belief that all the civilisations, which have ceased to be, have come by their death when the mind of the majority got killed under some pressure by the minority; for the truest wealth of man is his mind. No amount of respect outwardly accorded, can save man from the inherent ingloriousness of labour, divorced from mind. Only those who feel that they have become inwardly small can be belittled by others, and the numbers of the higher castes have ever dominated over those of the lower, not because they have any accidental advantage of power, but because the latter are themselves humbly conscious of their dwarfed humanity. If the cultivation of science by Europe has any moral significance, it is in its rescue of man from outrage by nature,—not its use of man as a machine, but its use of the machine to harness the forces of nature in man's service. One thing is certain, that the all-embracing poverty which has overwhelmed our country cannot he removed by working with our hands to the neglect of science. Nothing can be more undignified drudgery than that man's knowing should stop dead and his doing go on for ever.

It was a great day for man when he discovered the wheel. The facility of motion thus given to inert matter enabled it to bear much of man's burden. This was but right, for Matter is the true Shudra; while with his dual existence in body and mind, Man is a *Dwija*. Man has to maintain both his inner and outer life. Whatever functions he cannot perform by material means, are left as an additional burden on himself, bringing him to this extent down to the level of matter, and making him a Shudra. Such Shudras cannot obtain glory by being merely glorified in words.

Thus, whether in the shape of the spinning wheel, or the potter's wheel or the wheel of a vehicle, the wheel has rescued innumerable men from the Shudra's estate and lightened their burdens. No wealth is greater than this lightening of man's material burdens. This fact man has realised ever more and more, since the time when he turned his first wheel; for his wealth has thereupon gone on compounding itself in ever-increasing rotation, refusing to be confined to the limited advantage of the original *Charkha.*

Is there no permanent truth underlying these facts? One aspect of Vishnu's *shakti* is the *Padma*, the beautiful lotus; another is the *Chakra*, the movable discus. The one is the complete ideal of perfection, the other is the process of movement, the ever-active power seeking fulfilment. When man attained touch with this moving *shakti* of Vishnu, he was liberated from that inertia which is the origin of all poverty. All divine power is infinite. Man has not yet come to the end of the power revolving wheel. So, if we are taught that in the pristine *Charkha* we have exhausted all the means of spinning thread, we shall not gain the full favour of Vishnu. Neither will his spouse Lakshmi smile on us. When we forget that science is spreading the domain of Vishnu's *Chakra*, those who have honoured to Discus-bearer to better purpose will spread their dominion over us. If we are wilfully blind to the grand vision of whirling forces, which science has revealed, the *Charkha* will cease to have any message for us. The hum of the spinning wheel which, once carried us so long a distance on the path of wealth, will no longer talk to us of progress.

Some have protested that they ever preached that only the turning of *Charkha* should be engaged in. But they have not spoken of any other necessary work. Only one means of attaining *Swaraj* has been definitely ordered and the rest is a vast silence. Does not such silence amount to a speech stronger than any uttered word? Is not the *Charkha* thrust out against the background of this silence into undue prominence? Is it really so big as all that? Has it really the divinity which may enable it to appropriate the single-minded devotion of all the millions of India, despite their diversity of temperament and talent? Repeated efforts, even unto violence and bloodshed, have been made, all the world over, to bring mankind together on the basis of the common worship of a common Deity. But even these have not been successful. Neither has a common God been found, nor a common form of worship. Can it then be expected, that in the shrine of *Swaraj*, the *Charkha* goddess will attract to herself alone the offerings of every devotee? Surely such expectation amounts to a distrust of human nature, a disrespect for India's people.

In my childhood, I had an up-country servant, called *Gopee*, who used to tell us how once he went to Puri on a pilgrimage, and was at a loss what fruit to offer to Jagannath, since any fruit so offered could not be eaten by him any more. After repeatedly going over the list of edible fruits known to him, he suddenly bethought himself of the tomato, and the tomato it was which he offered, never having reason to repent of such clever abnegation. But to call upon man to make the easiest of offerings to the smallest of gods is the greatest of insults to his manhood. To ask all the millions of our people to spin the *Charkha* is as bad as offering the tomato to Jagannath. I do hope and trust that there are not thirty-three crores of *Gopees* in India.

When man receives the call of the great to make some sacrifice, he is indeed exalted; for then he comes to himself with a start of revelation,—to find that he too has been bearing his hidden resource of greatness.

Our country is the land of rites and ceremonials, so that we have more faith in worshipping the feet of the priest than the Divinity whom he serves. We cannot get rid of the conviction that we can safely cheat our innerself of its claims, if we can but bribe some outside agency. This reliance on outward help is a symptom of slavishness, for no habit can more easily destroy all reliance on self. Only to such a country can come the *Charkha* as the emblem of her deliverance; and the people, dazed into obedience by some specious temptation, go on turning their *Charkha* in the seclusion of their corners, dreaming all the while that the car of *Swaraj* of itself rolls onward in triumphal progress at every turn of their wheel.

And so it becomes necessary to restate afresh the old truth that the foundation of *Swaraj* cannot be based on any external conformity, but only on the internal union of hearts. If a great union is to be achieved, its field must be great likewise. But if, out of the whole field of economic endeavour, only one fractional portion be selected for special concentration thereon, then we may get home-spun thread, and even genuine *Khaddar*, but we shall not have united, in the pursuit of one great complete purpose, the lives of our countrymen.

In India, it is not possible for every one to unite in the realm of religion. The attempt to unite on the political platform is of recent growth, and will yet take long to permeate the masses. So that the religion of economics is where we should above all try to bring about this union of ours. It is certainly the largest field available to us; for here high and low, learned and ignorant, all have their scope. If this field cease to be one of welfare, if there we can prove that not competition, but cooperation is the real truth, then indeed we can reclaim from the hands of the evil one, an immense territory for the reign of peace and good will. It is important to remember, moreover, that this is the ground whereon our village communities had actually practised unity in the past. What if the thread of the old union has snapped? It may again be joined together; for such former practice has left in our character the potentiality of its renewal.

As is livelihood for the individual, so is politics for a particular people,—a field for the exercise of their business instincts of patriotism. All this time, just as business has implied antagonism, so has politics been concerned with the self-interest of a pugnacious nationalism. The forging of arms and of false documents has been its main activity. The burden of competitive armaments has been increasing space, with no end to it in sight, no peace for the world in prospect.

When it becomes clear to man that in the cooperation of nation lies the true interest of each,—for man is established in mutuality—then only can politics become a field for true endeavour. Then will the same means which the individual recognises as moral and therefore true, be also recognised as such by the nations. They will know that cheating, robbery and the exclusive pursuit of self-aggrandisement are as harmful for those of the next. It may be that the League of Nations will prove to be the first step in the process of this realisation.

Again just as the present-day politics is a manifestation of extreme individualism in nations, so is the process of gaining a livelihood an expression of the extreme selfishness of individuals. That is why man has descended to such depths of deceit and cruelty in his indiscriminate competition. And yet, since man is man, even in his business he ought to have cultivated his humanity rather than the powers of exploitation. In working for his livelihood he ought to have earned not only his daily bread, but also his eternal truth.

When, years ago, I first became acquainted with the principles of cooperation in the field of business, one of the knots of a tangled problem which had long perplexed my mind seemed to have been unravelled. I felt the separateness of self-interest, which had so long contemptuously ignored the claims of the truth of man, was at length to be replaced by a combination of common interest which would help to uphold that truth, proclaiming that poverty lay in the separation, and wealth in the union of man and man. For myself I had never believed that this original truth of man could find its limit in any region of his activity.

The co-operative principle tells us, in the fields of man's livelihood, that only when he arrives at his truth, can he get rid of his poverty,—not by any external means. And the manhood of man is at length honoured by the enunciation of this principle. Co-operation is an ideal, not a mere system and therefore it can give rise to innumerable methods of its application. It leads us into no blind ally; for at every step it communes with our spirit. And so, it seemed to me, in its wake would come, not merely food, but the goddess of plenty herself, in whom all kinds of material food are established in an essential moral oneness.

It was while some of us were thinking of the ways and means

of adopting this principle in our institution that I came across the book called *The National Being* written by that Irish idealist, A.E., who has a rare combination in himself of poetry and practical wisdom. There I could see a great concrete realisation of the cooperative living of my dreams. It became vividly clear to me what varied results could flow therefrom, how full the life of man could be made thereby. I could understand how great the concrete truth was in any plan of life, the truth that in separation is bondage, in union is liberation. It has been said in the *Upanishads* that Brahma is reason, Brahmo is spirit, but *Anna* also is Brahma, which means that Food also represents an eternal truth, and therefore through it we may arrive at a great realisation, if we travel along the true path.

I know there will be many to tax me with indicating a solution of great difficulty. To give concrete shape to the ideal of co-operation on so vast a scale will involve endless toil in experiment and failure, before at length it may become an accomplished fact. No doubt it is difficult. Nothing great can be cheap. We only cheat ourselves when we try to acquire things that are precious with a price that is inadequate. The problem of our poverty being complex, with its origin in our ignorance and unwisdom, in the inaptitude of our habits, the weakness of our character, it can only be effectively attacked by taking in hand our life as a whole and finding both internal and external remedies for the malady which afflicts it. How can there be an easy solution?

There are many who assert and some who believe that *Swaraj* can be attained by the *Charkha*. But I have yet to meet a person who has a clear idea of the process. That is why there is no discussion, but only quarreling over the question. If I state that it is not possible to repel foreign invaders armed with guns and cannons by the indigenous bow and arrow, there will, I suppose, be still some to contradict me asking, 'Why not?' It has already been said by some, 'Would not the foreigners be drowned, even if every one of our three hundred and thirty millions were only to spit at them?' While not denying the fearsomeness of such a flood, or the efficacy of such a suggestion, for throwing odium on foreign military science, the difficulty, which my mind feels to be insuperable, is that you can never get all these millions even to spit in unison. It is too simple for human beings. The same difficulty applies to the *Charkha* solution.

The disappointments, the failures, the recommencement that Sir Horace Plunkett had to face when he set to work to apply the cooperative principle in the economic reconstruction of Ireland, are a matter of history. But though it takes time to start a fire, once alight it spreads rapidly. That is the way with truth as well. In whatever corner of the earth it may take root, the range of its seeds is world-wide, and everywhere they find soil for growth and give of their fruit to each locality. Sir Horace Plunkett's success was not confined to Ireland alone; he achieved also the possibility of success for India. If any true devotee of our motherland should be able to eradicate the poverty of only one of her villages, he will have given permanent wealth to the thirty-three crores of his countrymen. Those who are won't to measure truth by its size get only an outside view, and fail to realise that each seed, in its tiny vital spark, brings divine authority to conquer the whole world.

As I am writing this, a friend objects that even though I may be right in thinking that the *Charkha* is not competent to bring us *Swaraj*, or remove the whole of our poverty, why ignore such virtues as it admittedly possesses? Every farmer, every householder, has a great deal of leisure left over after his ordinary work is done; so that if everyone would utilise such spare time in productive work much could be done towards the alleviation of our poverty. Why not glorify the *Charkha* as one of the instruments of such a desirable consummation? This reminds me of a similar proposition I have heard before. Most of our people throw away the water in which their rice is boiled. If everyone conserved this nutritious fluid that would go a long way to solve the food problem. I admit there is truth in this contention. The slight change of taste, required for eating boiled rice with its water retained, should not be very difficult to acquire, in view of the object sought to be gained. Many other similar savings could be effected which are doubtless worth the effort and should be looked upon as a duty. But has any one ever suggested that the conservation of rice-water should be made a plank in the platform of *Swaraj* work? And is there no good reason for the commission?

In order to make my point clear let me take an instance from the case of religion. If a preacher should repeatedly and insistently urge that the drinking of water from any and every well is the cause of the degeneracy of our religion, then the chief objection to his teaching would be its tendency to debase the value of moral action as a factor in religion. No doubt there is the chance of some well or other containing impure water; impure water destroys health; a diseased body begets a diseased mind, and therefore spiritual welfare is in danger. I am not concerned to dispute the truth in all this, yet I must repeat that to give undue value to the comparatively unimportant, lowers the value of the important. And so we find that there are numbers of Hindus who would not hesitate even to kill a Mohamedan if he came to draw water from their own well. If the small be put on an equal footing with the big, it is not content to rest there, but needs must push its way higher up. That is how the injunction: 'Thou shall not drink dubious water', gets the better of the commandment, 'Thou shall not kill'. There is no end to the perversions of value which have thus weakened our minds, and it is only because we have become habituated to their facile intrusion that no one is surprised to see the *Charkha* stalk the land, with uplifted club, in the garb of *Swaraj* itself. The *Charkha* is doing harm because of undue prominence which it has thus usurped, whereby it only adds fuel to the smouldering weakness that is eating into our vitals. Suppose some mighty voice should next proclaim that the rice-water must not be suffered to enter our councils. Given requisite forcefulness, that may lead to the flow of rice-water being followed by the flow of human blood, in the sacred name of political purity. If the idea of the impurity of foreign textiles should effect a lodgement in our mind along with the numerous fixed ideas already there, in regard to the impurity of certain foods and waters, the *Id* riots, to which we are accustomed, might pale before the sanguinary strife that may eventually be set ablaze between the so-called unclean lot who may use foreign cloth and those politically pure souls who do not. The danger to my mind is that the contagion of 'untouchability', which was hitherto confined to our society, may extend to the economic and political spheres as well.

Some one whispers to me that to combine in *Charkha* spinning in co-operation itself. I beg to disagree. If all the higher caste people of the Hindu community combine in keeping their well-water undefiled from use of the lower ones, this practice in itself does not give it the dignity of bacteriology. It is a particular action isolated from the comprehensive vision of this science. And therefore while we keep our wells reserved for the cleaner sect, we allow our ponds to get polluted, the ditches round our houses to harbour messengers of death. Those who intimately know Bengal also know that at the time of preparing a special kind of pickle our women take extra precaution in keeping themselves clean. In fact they go through a kind of ceremonial of ablution and other forms of purifications. For such extra care their pickle survives the ravage of time, while their villages are devastated by epidemics. For while there may remain some Pasteur's law invisible at the depth of this pickle-making precaution, the diseased spleens in the neighbourhood make themselves only too evident by their magnitude. The universal application of Pasteur's law in the production of pickle has some similarity to the application of the principle of a co-operation method of livelihood in turning the spinning wheel. It may produce enormous quantity of yarn, but the blind suppression of intellect which guards our poverty in its dark dungeon will remain violate. This narrow activity will shed light only upon one detached piece of fact, keeping its great background of truth densely dark.

It is extremely distasteful to me to have to differ from Mahatma Gandhi in regard to any matter of principle or method. Not that, from a higher standpoint, there is anything wrong in so doing; but my heart shrinks from it. For what could be a greater joy than to join hands in the fields of work with one for whom one have such love and reverence? Nothing is more wonderful to me than Mahatmaji's great moral personality. In him divine providence has given us a burning thunderbolt of *shakti*. May this *shakti* give power to India,—not overwhelm her,—that is my prayer! The difference in our standpoints and temperaments had made the Mahatma look upon Rammohun Roy as pygmy, while I revere him as a giant. The sáme difference makes the Mahatma's field of work one which my conscience cannot accept as its own. That is a regret which will abide with me always. It is, however, God's will that man's paths of endeavour shall be various, else why these differences of mentality? How often have my personal feelings of regard strongly urged me to accept at Mahatma Gandhi's hands my enlistment as a follower of the *Charkha* cult, but as often have my reason and conscience restrained me, lest I should be a party to the raising of the *Charkha* to a higher place than is its due, thereby distracting attention from other more important factors in our task of all-round reconstruction. I feel sure that Mahatmaji himself will not fail to understand me, and keep for me the same forbearance which he has always had. Acharya Ray, I also believe, has respect for independence of opinion, even when unpopular; so that, although when carried away by the fervour of his own propaganda he may now and then give me a scolding, I doubt not he retains for me a soft corner in his heart. As for my countrymen, the public—accustomed as they are to down, under the facile flow of their minds both past services and past disservices done to them,—if today they cannot find it in their hearts to forgive, they will forget tomorrow. Even if they do not,—if for me their displeasure is fated to be permanent, then just as today I have Acharya Seal as my fellow culprit, so tomorrow I may find at my side persons rejected by their own country whose radiance reveals the black unreality of any stigma of popular disapprobation.

Gandhi replied to Tagore through his article 'The Poet and the *Charkha*' in *Young India*: When Sir Rabindranath's criticism of the *Charkha* was published some time ago, several friends asked me to reply to it. Being heavily engaged I was unable then to study it in full. But I had read enough of it to know its trend. I was in no hurry to reply. Those who had read it were too much agitated or influenced to be able to appreciate what I might have been written even if I had the time. Now therefore is really the time for me to write on it and to ensure a dispassionate view being taken of the Poet's criticism or my reply if such it may be called.

The criticism is a sharp rebuke to Acharya Ray for his impatience of the Poet's and Acharya Seal's position regarding the *Charkha*, and a gentle rebuke to me for my exclusive and excessive love of it. Let the public understand that the Poet does not deny its great economic value. Let them know that he signed the appeal for the All-India Deshabandhu Memorial after he had written his criticism. He signed the appeal after studying its contents carefully and even as he signed it he sent me the message that he had written something on the *Charkha* which might not quite please me. I knew therefore what was coming. But it has not displeased me. Why should mere disagreement with my views displease? If every disagreement were to displease, since no two men agree exactly on all points, life would be a bundle of unpleasant sensations and therefore a perfect nuisance. On the contrary the frank criticism pleases me. For our friendship becomes all the richer for our disagreements. Friends to be friends are not called upon to agree even on most points. Only disagreement must have no sharpness, much less bitterness, about them. And I gratefully admit that there is none about the Poet's criticism.

I am obliged to make these prefatory remarks as dame rumour has whispered that jealousy is the root of all that criticism. Such baseless suspicion betrays an atmosphere of weakness and intolerance. A little reflection must remove all ground for such a cruel charge. Of what should the Poet be jealous in me? Jealousy presupposes the possibility of rivalry. Well, I have never succeeded in writing a single rhyme in my life. There is nothing of the Poet about me. I cannot aspire after his greatness. He is the undisputed master of it. The world today does not possess his equal as a poet. My Mahatmaship has no relation to the poet's undisputed position. It is time to realise that our fields are absolutely different and at no point overlapping. The Poet lives in a magnificent world of his own creation—his world of idea. I am a slave of somebody else's creation—the spinning wheel. The Poet makes his *gopis* dance to the tune of his flute. I wander after my beloved Sita, the *Charkha*, and seek to deliver her from the ten-headed monster from Japan, Manchester, Paris, etc. The Poet is an inventor, he creates, destroys and recreates. I am an explorer and having discovered a thing I must cling to it. The Poet present the world with new and attractive things from day to day. I can merely show the hidden possibilities of old and even worn out things. The world easily finds an honourable place for the magician who produces new and dazzling things. I have to struggle laboriously to find a corner for my worn out things. There is thus no competition between us. But I may say in all humility that we complement each other's activity.

The fact is that the Poet's criticism is a poetic licence and he who takes it literally is in danger of finding himself in an awkward corner. An ancient poet has said that Solomon arrayed in all his glory was not like one of the lilies of the field. He clearly referred to the natural beauty and innocence of the lily contrasted with the artificiality of Solomon's glory and his sinfulness in spite of his many good deeds. Or take the poetical licence in 'It is easier for a camel to pass through the eye of a needle than for a rich man to enter the Kingdom of Heaven'. We know that no camel has ever passed through the eyes of a needle and we know too that rich men like Janaka have entered the Kingdom of Heaven. Or take the beautiful smile of human teeth being likened to the pomegranate seed. Foolish women who have taken the poetical exaggeration literally have been found to disfigure and even harm their teeth. Painters and poets are obliged to exaggerate the proportions of their figures in order to give true perspective. Those therefore who take the Poet's denunciation of the *Charkha* literally will be doing an injustice to the Poet and an injury to themselves.

The Poet does not, he is not expected, he had no need, to read *Young India*. All he knows about the movement is what he has picked up from table-talk. He has therefore denounced what he imagined to be the excesses of the *Charkha*.

He thinks, for instance, that I want everybody to spin the whole of his or her time to the exclusion of all other activity, that is to say, that I want the Poet to forsake his muse, the farmer his plough, the lawyer his brief and the doctor his lancet. So far is this from truth that I have asked no one to abandon his calling, but on the contrary to adorn it by giving every day only thirty minutes to spinning as sacrifice for the whole nation. I have indeed asked the famishing man or woman who is idle for want of any work whatsoever to spin for a living and the half-starved farmer to spin during his leisure hours to supplement his slender resources. If the Poets span half an hour daily his poetry would gain in richness. For it would then represent the poor man's wants and woes in a more forcible manner than now.

The Poet thinks that the *Charkha* is calculated to bring about a deathlike sameness in the nation and thus imagining he would shun it if he could. The truth is that the *Charkha* is intended to realise the essential and living oneness of interest among India's myriads. Behind the magnificent and kaleidoscopic variety one discovers in nature a unity of purpose, design and form which is equally unmistakable. No two men are absolutely alike, not even twins, and yet there is much that is indispensably common to all mankind. And behind the commonness of form there is the same life pervading all. The idea of sameness or oneness was carried by Shankara to its utmost logical and natural limit and he exclaimed that there was only one Truth, one God-Brahman and all form, *nama*, *rupa* was illusion or illusory, evanescent. We need not debate whether what we see is unreal; and whether the real behind the unreality is what we do not see. Let both be equally real if you will. All I say is that there is sameness, identity or oneness behind the multiplicity and variety. And so do I hold that behind a variety of occupations there is an indispensable sameness also of occupation. Is not agriculture common to the vast majority of mankind? Even so was spinning common not long ago to a vast majority of mankind. Just as both prince and peasant must eat and clothe themselves, so must both labour for supplying their primary wants. The prince may do so if only by way of symbol and sacrifice but that much is indispensable for him if he will be true to himself and his people. Europe may not realise this vital necessity at the present moment, because it has made of exploitation of non-European races a religion. But it is a false religion bound to perish in the near future. The non-European races will not for ever allow themselves to be exploited. I have endeavoured to show a way out that is peaceful, humane and therefore noble. It may be rejected. If it is, the alternative is a tug-of-war, in which each will try to pull down the other. Then when non-Europeans will seek to exploit the Europeans, the Truth of the *Charkha* will have to be realised. Just as, if we are to live we must breathe, not air imported from England nor eat food so imported, so may we not import cloth even from Bombay or from Benga Lakshmi. If Bengal will live her natural and free life without exploiting the rest of India or the world outside, she must manufacture her cloth in her own villages as she grows her corn there. Machinery has its place; it has come to stay. But it must not be allowed to displace the necessary human labour. An improved plough is a good thing. But if by some chance one man could plough up by some mechanical invention of his the whole of the land of India and control all the agricultural produce and if the millions had no other occupation, they would starve, and being idle, they would become dunces, as many have already become. There is hourly danger of many more being reduced to that inevitable state. I would welcome every improvement in the cottage machine; but I know it is criminal to displace the hand labour by the introduction of power-driven spindles, unless one is at the same time ready to give millions of farmers some other occupations in their homes.

The Irish analogy does not take us very far. It is perfect insofar as it enables us to realise the necessity of economic cooperation. But Indian circumstances being different, the method of working out cooperation is necessarily different. For Indian distress every effort at cooperation has to centre round the *Charkha* if it is to apply to the majority of the inhabitants of this vast Peninsula, 1900 miles long and 1500 miles broad. A Sir Gangaram may give us a model farm which can be no model for the penniless Indian farmer who has hardly two to three acres of land which every day runs the risk of being still further cut up.

Round the *Charkha*, that is, amidst the people who have shed their idleness and who have understood the value of cooperation, a national servant would build up a programme of anti-malaria campaign, improved sanitation, settlement of village disputes, conservation and breeding of cattle and hundreds of other beneficial activities. Wherever *Charkha* work is fairly established, all such ameliorative activity is going on, according to the capacity of the villages and the workers concerned.

It is not my purpose to traverse all the Poet's arguments in detail. Where the differences between us are not fundamental,—and these I have endeavoured to state,—there is nothing in the Poet's argument which I cannot endorse and still maintain my position regarding the *Charkha*. The many things about the *Charkha* which he has ridiculed I have never said. The merits I have claimed for the *Charkha* remain undamaged by the Poet's battery.

One thing, and one thing only, has hurt me, the Poet's belief, again picked up from table-talk, that I look upon Rammohan Roy as a Pigmy! Well, I have never anywhere described that great reformer as a pigmy, much less regarded him as such. He is to me as much a giant as he is to the Poet. I do not remember any occasion save one when I had to use Rammohan Roy's name. That was in connection with Western education. This was on the Cuttack sands now four years ago. What I do remember having said was that it was possible to attain highest culture without Western education. And when some one mentioned Rammohun Roy, I remember having said that he was a pigmy compared to the unknown authors, say of the *Upanishads*. This is altogether different from looking upon Rammohun Roy as a pigmy. I do not think meanly of Tennyson if I say that he was a pigmy before Milton or Shakespeare. I claim that I enhance the greatness of both. If I adore the Poet as he knows I do, in spite of differences between us, I am not likely to disparage the greatness of the man who made the great reform movement of Bengal possible and of which the Poet is one of the finest of fruits.

On reading this article Tagore wrote a letter to Gandhiji assuring him that 'even if you have hit me hard in the cause of what you think is Truth, our personal relationship based upon mutual respect will bear that strain'.

5

ON NON-COOPERATION MOVEMENT

From Europe, Tagore expressed his anxiety to friends in India and three of his letters appeared in *Modern Review*. He had his doubts about the non-cooperation movement. The three letters clearly reveal his opinions on the feasibility of non-cooperation movement. He wrote the first letter to Gandhiji on 12th April, 1919 from Shantiniketan: Power in all its forms is irrational, it is like the horse that drags the carriage blind-folded. The moral element in it is only represented in the man who drives the horse. Passive resistance is a force which is not necessarily moral in itself, it can be used against truth as well as for it. The danger inherent in all force grows stronger when it is likely to gain success, for then it becomes temptation.

I know your teaching is to fight against evil by the help of the good. But such a fight is for heroes and not for men led by the impulses of the moment. Evil on one side naturally begets evil on the other, injustice leading to violence and insult to revengefulness. Unfortunately such a force has already been started and either through panic or through wrath, or authorities have shown us their claws whose sure effect is to drive some of us into the secret path of resentment and others into utter demoralisation.

In this crisis you, as a great leader of men, have stood among us to proclaim your faith in the ideal which you know to be that of India, the ideal which is both against the cowardliness of hidden revenge and the coward submissiveness of the terror-stricken. You have said, as Lord Buddha had done in his time and for all time to come: Conquer anger by the power of non-anger evil by the power of good.

This power of good must prove its truth and strength by its fearlessness, by its refusal to accept any imposition which depends for its success, upon its power to produce frightfulness and is not ashamed to use its machines of destruction to terrorise a people completely disarmed. We must know that moral conquest does not consist in success, that failure does not deprive it of its dignity and worth. Those who believe in spiritual life know that to stand against wrong which has overwhelming material power behind it is victory itself, it is the victory of the active faith in the ideal in the teeth of evident defeat.

I have always feet, and said accordingly, that the great gift of freedom can never come to a people through charity. We must win it before we can own it. And India's opportunity for winning it will come to her when she can prove that she is morally superior to the people who rule her by their right of conquest. She must willingly accept her penance of suffering, the suffering which is the crown of the great. Armed with her utter faith in goodness she must stand unabashed before the arrogance that scoffs the power of spirit.

And you have come to your motherland in the time of her need to remind her of her mission, to lead her in the true path of conquest, to purge her present-day politics of its feebleness which imagines that it has gained its purpose when it sturts in the borrowed feathers of diplomatic dishonesty.

This is why I pray most fervently that nothing that tends to weaken our spiritual freedom may intrude into your marching line, that martyrdom mist, that will vanish, leaving no stain on the radiance of the Eternal. However, we may delude ourselves with the phrases learnt from the West, *Swaraj* is not our objective. Our fight is a spiritual fight . . . it is for Man. We are to emancipate Man from the meshes that he himself has woven round him . . . these organisations of National Egoism. The butterfly will have to be persuaded that the freedom of the sky is of higher value than the shelter of the cocoon. If we can defy the strong, the armed, the wealthy . . . revealing to the world the power of the immortal spirit, the whole castle of the Great Flesh will vanish in the void. And then Man will find his *Swaraj*. We, the famished, ragamuffins of the East, are to win freedom, for all Humanity. We have no word for 'Nation' in our language. When we borrow this word from other people, it never fits us. For we are to make our league with Narayana, and our victory will not give us anything but victory itself; victory for God's world. I have seen the West; I covet not the unholy feast, in which she revels every moment, growing more and more bloated and red and dangerously delirious. Not for us, is the mad orgy of midnight, with lighted torches, but awakenment in the serene light of morning.

Tagore called the concept of non-cooperation as political asceticism in his letter of 5 March, 1925. He wrote: The idea of non-cooperation is political asceticism. Our students are bringing their offering of sacrifices to what? Not to a fuller education, but to non-education. It has at its back a fierce joy of annihilation which at its best is asceticism, and at its worst is that orgy of frightfulness in which the human nature, losing faith in the basic reality of normal life, finds a disinterested delight in an unmeaning devastation, as has been shown in the late war and on other occasion which came nearer to us. No in its passive moral form is ascesticism and in its active moral form is violence. The desert is as much a form of *himsa* as is the raging sea in storm; they both are against life.

I remember the day during the *Swadeshi* movement in Bengal, when a crowd of young students came to see me in the first floor hall of our Vichitra house. They said to me that if I would order them to leave their schools and colleges they would instantly oblige. I was emphatic in my refusal to do so, and they went away angry, doubting the sincerity of my love for my motherland. And yet long before this popular ebullition of excitement I myself had given a thousand rupees, when I had not five rupees to call my own, to open a *Swadeshi* store and courted banter and bankruptcy. The reason of my refusing to advise those students to leave their schools was because the anarchy of a mere emptiness never tempts me, even when it is resorted to as a temporary measure. I am frightened of an abstraction which is ready to ignore living reality. . . . You know that I do not believe in the material civilisation of the West just as I do not believe in the physical body to be the highest truth in man. But I still less believe in the destruction of the physical body, and the ignoring of the material necessities of life. What is needed is establishment of harmony between the physical and spiritual nature of man, maintaining of balance between the foundation and superstructure. I believe in the true meeting of the East and the West. Love is the ultimate truth of soul. We should do all we can, not to outrage that truth, to carry its banner against all opposition. The idea of non-cooperation unnecessarily hurts that truth. It is not our hearth fire, but the fire that burns out our hearth and home.

In his letter of 13 March, 1921, Tagore wrote: Today at this critical moment of the world's history, cannot India rise above her limitations and offer the great ideal to the world that will work towards harmony in cooperation between the different peoples of the earth? Men of faith will say that India requires to be strong and right before she can raise her voice for the sake of the whole world. But I refuse to believe it.

That the measure of man's greatness is in his material resources is a gigantic illusion casting its shadow over the present day world—it is an insult to man. It lies in the power of the materially weak to save the world from this illusion and India in spite of her penury and humiliation, can afford to come to the rescue of humanity.

The idea of India is against the intense consciousness of the separateness of one's own people from others, and which inevitably leads to ceaseless conflicts. Therefore my one prayer is, let India stand for cooperation of all peoples of the world. The spirit of rejection finds its support in the consciousness of separation, the spirit of acceptance in the consciousness of unity. India has ever declared that Unity is truth, and separateness is *maya.* This unity is not a zero, it is that which comprehends all and therefore can never be reached through the path of negation. Our present struggle to alienate our heart and mind from those of the West is an attempt at spiritual suicide. If in the spirit of national vain-gloriousness we shout from our housetops that the West has produced nothing that has an infinite velour for man, then we but create a serious cause of doubt about the worth of any product of the Eastern mind. For it is the mind of man in the East and West which is ever approaching Truth in her different aspects from different angles of vision; and if it can be true that the strength of West has betrayed it into an utter misdirection, than we can never be sure of the standpoint of the East. Let us be rid of all false pride and rejoice at any lamp being lit at any corner of the world, knowing that it is a part of the common illumination of our house.

The West has misunderstood the East which is at the root of the disharmony that prevails between them. But will it mend the matter if the East in her turn tries to misunderstand the West? The present age has powerfully been possessed by the West; it has only become possible because to her is given some great mission for man. We from the East have to come to her to learn whatever she has to teach us; for by doing so we hasten the fulfilment of this age. We know that the East also has her lessons to give, and she has her own responsibility of not allowing her light to be extinguished, and the time will come when the West will find leisure to realise that she has a home of hers in the East where her food is and her rest.

Gandhiji replied to Tagore's charge in the *Young India* on 1 June, 1921 under the title 'The Poet's Anxiety' as follows: The Poet of Asia, as Lord Hardinge called Dr. Tagore, is fast becoming, if he has not already become the Poet of the world. Increasing prestige has brought to him increasing responsibility. His greatest service to india must be his poetic interpretation of India's message to the world. The Poet is therefore sincerely anxious that India should deliver no false or feeble message in her name. He is naturally jealous of his country's reputation. He says he has striven hard to find himself in tune with the present movement. He confesses that he is baffled. He can find nothing for his lyre in the din and the bustle of non-cooperation. In three forceful letters, he has endeavoured to give expression to his misgivings and he has come to the conclusion that non-cooperation is not dignified enough for the India of his vision, that it is a doctrine of negation and despair. He fears that it is a doctrine of separation, exclusiveness, narrowness and negation.

No Indian can feel anything but pride in the Poet's exquisite jealousy of India's honour. It is good that he should have sent to us his misgivings in language at once beautiful and clear.

In all humility, I shall endeavour to answer the Poet's doubts. I may fail to convince him or the reader who may have been touched by his eloquence, but I would like to assure him and India that non-cooperation in conception is not any of the things he fears, and he need have no cause to be ashamed of his country for having adopted non-cooperation. If, in actual application, it appears in the end to have failed, it will be no more the fault of the doctrine, that it would be of Truth, if those who claim to apply it in practice do not appear to succeed. Non-cooperation may have come in advance of its time. India and the world must then wait, but there is no choice for India save between vioience and non-cooperation.

Nor need the Poet fear that non-cooperation is intended to erect a Chinese wall between India and the West. On the contrary, non-cooperation is intended to pave the way to real, honourable and voluntary cooperation based on mutual respect and trust. The present struggle is being waged against compulsory cooperation, against one sided combination, against the armed imposition of modern methods of exploitation masquerading under the name of civilisation.

Non-cooperation is a protest against an unwitting and unwilling participation in evil. The Poet's concern is largely about the students. He is of the opinion that they should not have been called upon to give up Government schools before they had other schools to go to. Here I must differ from him. I have never been able to make a fetish of literary training. My experience has proved to my satisfaction that literary training by itself adds not an inch to one's moral height and that character-building is independent of literary training. I am firmly of opinion that the Government schools have unmanned us, rendered us helpless and Godless. They have filled us with discontent, and, providing no remedy for the discontent, have made us despondent. They have made us what we were intended to become–clerks and interpreters. A government builds its prestige upon the apparently voluntary association of the governed. And if it was wrong to cooperate with the Government in keeping us slaves, we were bound to begin with those institutions in which our association appeared to be most voluntary. The youth of a nation are its hope. I hold that, as soon as we discovered that the system of Government was wholly, or mainly evil, it became sinful for us to associate our children with it.

It is no argument against the soundness of the proposition laid down by me that the vast majority of the students went back after the first flush of enthusiasm. Their recantation is proof rather of the extent of our degradation than of the wrongness of the step. Experience has shown that the establishment of national schools has not resulted in drawing many more students. The strongest and the truest of them came out without any national schools to fall back upon, and I am convinced that these first withdrawals are rendering service of the highest order.

But the Poet's protest against the calling out of the boys is really a corollary to his objection to the very doctrine of non-cooperation. He has a horror of everything negative. His whole soul seems to rebel against the negative commandments of religion. I must give his objection in his own inimitable language. Though I know it to be a fact, I cannot take it as a truth. *Brahmavidya* in India has for its object *mukti*, while Buddhism has *nirvana. Mukti* draws our attention to the positive and *nirvana* to the negative side of Truth. Therefore, he emphasized the fact of *dukha* which has to be avoided and the *Brahmavidya* emphasised the fact of *ananda* which had to be attained. In these passages, the reader will find the key to the Poet's mentality. In my humble opinion, rejection is as much an ideal as the acceptance of a thing. It is as necessary to reject untruth as it is to accept truth. All religions teach the two opposite forces act upon us and that the human endeavour consists in a series of eternal rejections and acceptances. Non-cooperation with evil is as much a duty as cooperation with good. I venture to suggest that the Poet has done an unconscious injustice to Buddhism in describing *nirvana* as merely a negative state. I make bold to say that *mukti* is as much a negative state as *nirvana*. Emancipation from or extinction of the bondage of the flesh leads to *ananda*. Let me close this part of my argument by drawing attention to the fact that the final word of the *Upanishads* is not. *Neti* was the best description the authors of the *Upanishads* were able to find for Brahman.

I therefore think that the Poet has been unnecessarily alarmed at the negative aspect of non-cooperation. We had lost the power of saying 'No'. It had become disloyal, almost sacrilegious to say 'no' to the government. This deliberate refusal to cooperate is like the necessary weeding process that a cultivator has to resort to before he sows. Weeding is as necessary to agriculture as sowing. Indeed, even whilst the crops are growing, the weeding fork, as every husbandman knows, is an instrument almost of daily use. The nation's non-cooperation is an invitation to the Government to cooperate with it on its own terms as is every nation's right and every good government's duty. Non-cooperation is the nation's notice that it is no longer satisfied to be in tutelage. The nation has taken to the harmless, natural and religious doctrine of non-cooperation in the place of the unnatural and irreligious doctrine of violence. And if India is ever to attain the *Swaraj* of the Poet's dream, she will do so only by non-cooperation. Let him deliver his message of peace to the world, and feel confident that India, through her non-cooperation, if she remains true to her pledge, will have exemplified his message. Non-cooperation is intended to give the very meaning to patriotism that the Poet is yearning after. An India prostrate at the feet of Europe can give no hope to humanity. An India awakened and free has a message of peace and goodwill to a groaning world. Non-cooperation is designed to supply her with a platform from which she will preach the message.

Tagore published in an English version in the *Modern Review* of October, 1921 under the title 'The Call of Truth'. It read: Parasities have to pay for their ready-made victuals by losing the power of assimilating food in natural form. In the history of man this same sin of laziness has always entailed degeneracy. Man becomes parasitical, not only when he faltens on others, toil, but also when he becomes rooted to a particular set of outside conditions and allows himself helplessly to drift along the stream of things as they are; for the outside is alien to the inner self, and if the former be made indispensable by sheer habit, man acquires parasitical characteristics, and becomes unable to perform his true function of converting the impossible into the possible.

In this sense all the lower animals are parasites. They are carried along by their environment; they live or die by natural selection; they progress or retrogress as nature may dictate. Their mind has lost the power of growth. The bees, for millions of years, have been unable to get beyond the pattern of their hive. For that reason, the form of their cell has attained a certain perfection, but their mentality is confined to the age-long habits of their hive-life and cannot soar out of its limitations. Nature has developed a cautious timidity in the case of her lower types of life; she keeps them tied to her apron strings and has stunted their minds, lest they should stray into dangerous experiments.

But Providence displayed a sudden accession of creative courage when it came to man; for his inner nature has not been tied down, though outwardly the poor human creature has been left naked, weak and defenceless. In spite of these disabilities, man in the joy of his inward freedom has stood up and declared: I shall achieve the impossible. That is to say, he has consistently refused to submit to the rule of things as they always have been, but is determined to bring about happenings that have never been before. So when, in the beginning of his history, man's lot was thrown in with monstrous creatures, tusked and taloned, he did not, like the deer, simply take refuge in flight, nor, like the tortoise, take refuge in hiding but set to work with flints to make even more efficient weapons. These, moreover, being the creation of his own inner faculties, were not dependent on natural selection, as were those of the other animals, for their development. And so man's instruments progressed from flint to steel. This shows that man's mind has never been helplessly attached to his environment. What came to his hand was brought under his thumb. Not content with the flint on the surface, he delved for the iron beneath. Not satisfied with the easier process of chipping flints, he proceeded to melt iron ore and hammer it into shape. That which resisted more stubbornly was converted, into a better ally. Man's inner nature not only finds success in its activity, but there it also has its joy. He insists on penetrating further and further into the depths, from the obvious to the hidden, from the easy to the difficult, from parasitism to self-determination, from the slavery of his passions to the mastery of himself. That is how he has won.

But if any section of mankind should say, "The flint was the weapon of our revered fore-fathers; by departing from it we destroy the spirit of the race", then they may succeed in preserving what they call their race, but they strike at the root of the glorious tradition of humanity which was theirs also. And we find that those, who have steadfastly stuck to their flint, may indeed have kept safe their pristine purity to their own satisfaction, but they have been out casted by the rest of mankind and so have to pass their lives slinking away in jungle and cave. They are, as I say, reduced to a parasitic dependence on outside nature, driven along blindfold by the force of things as they are. They have not achieved *Swaraj* in their inner nature, and so are deprived of *Swaraj* in the outside world as well. They have ceased to be even aware, that it is man's true function to make the impossible into the possible by dint of his own powers; that it is not for him to be confined merely to what has happend before; that he must progress towards what ought to be by rousing all his inner powers.by means of the force of his soul.

Thirty years ago I used to edit The *Sadhana* magazine and there I tried to say this same thing. Then English educated India was frightfully busy begging for its rights. And I repeatedly endeavoured to impress on my countrymen, that man is not under any necessity to beg for rights from others but must create them for himself; because man lives mainly by his inner nature, and there he is the master. By dependence on acquisition from the outside, man's inner nature suffers loss. And it was my contention, that man is not so hard oppressed by being deprived of his outward rights as he is by the constant bearing of the burden of prayers and petitions.

Then when *The Bangadarshan* magazine came into my hands, Bengal was beside herself at the sound of the sharpening of the knife for her partition. The boycott of Manchester, which was the outcome of her distress, had raised the profits of the Bombay mill-owners to a super-foreign degree. And I had then to say: This will not do, either, for it is also of the outside. Your main motive is hatred of the foreigner not love of country. It was then really necessary for our countrymen to be made conscious of the distinction, that the Englishman's presence is an external accident,—mere *maya*–but that the presence of our country is an internal fact which is also an eternal truth. *Maya* looms with an exaggerated importance, only when we fix our attention exclusively upon it, by reason of some infatuation—be it of love, or of hate. Whether in our passion we rush to embrace it, or attack it; whether we yearn for it, or spun it; it equally fills the whole field of our blood-shot vision.

Maya is like the darkness. No steed, however swift, can carry us beyond it; no amount of water can wash it away. Truth is like a lamp; even as it is lit, *maya* vanishes. Our *Shastras* tell us that Truth, even when it is small, can rescue us from the terror which is great. Fear is the atheism of the heart. It cannot be overcome from the side of negation. If one of its heads be struck off, it breeds, like the monster of the fable, a hundred others. Truth is positive; it is the affirmation of the soul. If even a little of it be roused, it attacks negation at the very heart and over-powers it wholly.

Alien Government in India is a veritable chameleon. Today it comes in the guise of the Englishman; tomorrow perhaps as some other foreigner; the next day, without abating a jot of its virulence, it may take the shape of our own countrymen. However determinedly we may try to hunt this monster of foreign dependence with outside lethal weapons, it will always elude our pursuit by changing its skin, or its colour. But if we can gain within us the truth called our country, all outward *maya* will vanish of itself. The declaration of faith that my country is there, to be realised, has to be attained by each one of us. The idea that our country is ours, merely because we have been born in it, can only be held by those who are fastened, in a parasitic existence, upon the outside world. But the true nature of man is his inner nature, with its inherent powers. Therefore, that only can be a man's true country, which he can help to create by his wisdom and will, his love and his actions. So in 1905, I called upon my countrymen to create their country by putting forth their own powers from within. For the act of creation itself is the realisation of truth.

The Creator gains Himself in His universe. To gain one's own country means to realise one's own soul more fully expanded within it. This can only be done when we are engaged in building it up with our service, our ideas and our activities. Man's country, being the creation of his own inner nature, when his soul thus expands within it, it is more truly expressed, more fully realised. In my paper called *Swadeshi Samaj*, written in 1905, I discussed at length the ways and means by which we could make the country of our birth more fully our own. Whatever may have been the shortcomings of my words then uttered, I did not fail to lay emphasis on the truth, that we must win our country, not from some foreigner, but from our own inertia, our own indifference. Whatever be the nature of the boons we may be seeking for our country at the door of the foreign Government, the result is always the same,—it only makes our inertia more densely inert. Any public benefit done by the alien Government goes to their credit, not to ours. So whatever outside advantage such public benefit might mean for us, our country will only get more and more completely lost to us thereby. That is to say, we shall have to pay out in soul value for what we purchase as material advantage. The Rishi has said:

"The son is dear, not because we desire a son, but because we desire to realise our own soul in him". It is the same with our country. It is dear to us, because it is the expressions of our own soul. When we realise this, it will become impossible for us to allow our service of our country to wait on the pleasure of others.

These truths, which I then tried to press on my countrymen, where not particularly new, nor was there anything therein which need have grated on their ears; but, whether anyone else remembers it or not, I at least am not likely to forget the storm of indignation which I roused. I am not merely referring to the hooligans of journalism whom it pays to be scurrilous. But even men of credit and courtesy were unable to speak of me in restrained language.

There were two root causes of this. One was anger, the second was greed.

Giving free vent to angry feelings is a species of a self-indulgence. In those days there was practically nothing to stand in the way of the spirit of destructive revel, which spread all over the country. We went about picketing, burning, placing thorns in the path of those whose way was not ours, acknowledging no restraints in language or behaviour,—all in the frenzy of our wrath. Shortly after, it was all over, a Japanese friend asked me: "How is it you people cannot carry on your work with calm and deep determination? This wasting of energy can hardly be of assistance to your object". I had no help but to reply: "When we have the gaining of the object clearly before our minds, we can be restrained, and concentrate our energies to serve it; but when it is a case of venting our anger, our excitement rises and rises till it drowns the object, and then we are spend thrift to the point of bankruptcy". However that may be, there were my countrymen encountering, for the time being, no check to the overflow of their outraged feelings. It was like a strange dream. Everything seemed possible. Then all of a sudden it was my misfortune to appear on the scene with my doubts and my attempts to divert the current into the path of self-determination. My only success was in diverting their wrath on to my own devoted head.

Then there was our greed. In history, all people have won valuable things by pursuing difficult paths. We had hit upon the device of getting them cheap, not even through the painful indignity of supplication with folded hands, but by proudly conducting our beggary in threatening tones. The country was in ecstasy at the ingenuity of the trick. It felt like being at a reduced price sale. Everything worth having in the political market was ticketed at half-price. Shabby-genteel mentality is so taken up with low prices that it has no attention to spare for quality, and feels inclined to attack anybody who has the hardihood to express doubts in that regard. It is like the man of worldly piety who believes that the judicious expenditure of coin can secure, by favour of the priest, a direct passage to heaven. The dare-devil who ventures to suggest that not heaven but dreamland is likely to be his destination, must beware of a violent end.

Anyhow, it was the outside *maya* which was our dream and our ideal in those days. It was a favourite phrase of cne of the leaders of the time that we must keep one hand at the feet and the other at the throat of the Englishman, —that is to say, with no hand left free for the country! We have since perhaps got rid of this ambiguous attitude. Now we have one party that has both hands down at his feet; but whichever attitude it may be, these methods still appertain to the outside *maya*. Our unfortunate minds keep revolving round and round the British Government, now to the left, now to the right; our affirmations and denials alike are concerned with the foreigner.

In those days, the stimulus from every side was directed towards the heart of Bengal. But emotion by itself, like fire, only consumes its fuel and reduces it to ashes; it has no creative power. The intellect of man must busy itself, with patience, with skill, with foresight, in using this fire to melt that which is hard and difficult into the object of its desire. We neglected to rouse our intellectual forces, and so were unable to make use of this surging emotion of ours to create any organisation of permanent value. The reason of our failure, therefore, was not in anything outside, but rather within us. For a long time past we have been in the habit, in our life and endeavour, of setting apart one place for our emotions and another for our practices. Our intellect has all the time remained dormant, because we have not dared to allow it scope. That is why, when we have to rouse ourselves to action, it is our emotion which has to be requisitioned, and our intellect has to be kept from interfering by the hypnotism of some magical formula,—that is to say we hasten to create a situation absolutely inimical to the free play of our intellect.

The loss which is incurred by this continual deadening of our mind cannot be made good by any other contrivance. In our desperate attempts to do so we have to invoke the magic of *maya* and our impotence jumps for joy at the prospect of getting hold of Aladin's lamp. Of course every one has to admit that there is nothing to beat Aladin's lamp, its only inconvenience being that it beats one to get hold of. The unfortunate part of it is that the person, whose greed is great, but whose powers are feeble, and who has lost all confidence in his own intellect, simply will not allow himself to dwell on the difficulties of bespeaking the services of some genie of the lamp. He can only be brought to exert himself at all by holding out the speedily prospect of getting at the wonderful lamp. If any one attempts to point out the futility of his hopes, he fills the air with wailing and imprecation, as at a robber making away with his all.

In the heat of the enthusiasm of the partition days a band of youths attempted to bring about the millennium through political revolution. Their offer of themselves as the first sacrifice to the fire which they had lighted makes not only their own country, but other countries as well, bare the head to them in reverence. Their physical failure shines forth as the effulgence of spiritual glory. In the midst of their supreme travail, they realised at length that the way of bloody revolution is not the trueway; that where there is no politics, a political revolution is like taking a shortcut to nothing; that the wrong way may appear shorter, but it does not reach the goal, and only grievously hurts the feet. The refusal to pay the full price for a thing leads to the loss of the price without the gain of the thing. These impetuous youths offered their lives as the price of their country's deliverance; to them it meant the loss of their all, but alas! the price offered on behalf of the country was insufficient. I feel sure that those of them who still survive must have realised by now, that the country must be the creation of all its people, not of one section alone. It must be the expression of all their forces of heart, mind and will.

This creation can only be the fruit of that *yoga*, which gives outward form to the inner faculties. Mere political or economical yoga is not enough; for that all the human powers must unite.

When we turn our gaze upon the history of other countries, the political steed comes prominently into view; on it seems to depend wholly the progress of the carriage. We forget that the carriage also must be in a fit condition to move; its wheels must be in agreement with one another and its parts well fitted together; with which not only have fire and hammer and chisel been busy but much thought and skill and energy have also been spent in the process. We have seen some countries which are externally free and independent; when, however, the political carriage is in motion, the noise which it makes arouses the whole neighbourhood from a slumber and the jolting produces aches and pains in the limbs of the helpless passengers. It comes to pieces in the middle of the road, and it takes the whole day to put it together again with the help of ropes and stings. Yet, however, loose the screws and however crooked the wheels, still it is a vehicle of some sort after all. But for such a thing as is our country,— a mere collection of jointed logs, that not only have no wholeness amongst themselves, but are contrary to one another,— for this to be dragged along a few paces by the temporary pull of some common greed or anger, can never be called by the name of political progress. Therefore, is it not, in our case, wiser to keep for the moment our horse in the stable and begin to manufacture a real carriage?

From the writings of the young men, who have come back out of the valley of the shadow of death, I feel sure some such thoughts must have occurred to them. And so they must be realising the necessity of the practice of yoga as of primary importance;— that form which is the union in a common endeavour of all the human faculties. This cannot be attained by any outside blind obedience, but only by the realisation of self in the light of intellect. That which fails to illumine the intellect, and only keeps it in the obsession of some delusion, is its greatest obstacle.

The call to make the country our own by dint of our own creative power, is a great call. It is not merely inducing the people to take up some external mechanical exercise; for man's life is not in making cells of uniform pattern like the bee, nor in incessant weaving of webs like the spider; his greatest powers are within, and on these are his chief reliance. If by offering some allurement we can induce man to cease from thinking, so that he may go on and on with some mechanical piece of work, this will only result on prolonging the sway of *maya*, under which our country has all along been languishing. So far, we have been content with surrendering our greatest right—the right to reason and to judge for ourselves—to the blind forces of shastric injunctions and social conventions. We have refused to cross the seas, because Manu has told us not to do so. We refuse to eat with the Mussalman, because prescribed usage is against it. In other words, we have systematically pursued a course of blind routine and habit, in which the mind of man has no place. We have thus been reduced to the helpless condition of the master who is altogether dependent on his servant. The real master, as I have said, is the internal man; and he gets into endless trouble, when he becomes his own servant's slave—a mere automation, manufactured in the factory of servitude. He can then only rescue himself from one master by surrendering himself to another. Similarly, he who glorifies inertia by attributing to it a fanciful purity, becomes, like it, dependent on outside impulses, both for rest and motion. The inertness of mind, which is the basis of all slavery, cannot be got rid of by a docile submission to being hoodwinked, nor by going through the motions of a wound-up mechanical doll.

The movement, which has now succeeded the *Swadeshi* agitation, is ever so much greater and has moreover extended its influence all over India. Previously, the vision of our political leaders had never reached beyond the English knowing classes, because the country meant for them only that bookish aspect of it which is to be found in the pages of the Englishman's history. Such a country was merely a mirage born of vapourings in the English language in which flitted about thin shades of Burke and Gladstone, Mazzini and Garibalde. Nothing resembling self-sacrifice or true feeling for their countrymen was visible. At this juncture, Mahatma Gandhi came and stood at the cottage door of the destitute millions, clad as one of themselves, and talking to them in their own language. Here was the truth at last, not a mere quotation out of a book. So the name of Mahatma, which was given to him, is his true name. Who else has felt so many men of India to be of his own flesh and blood? At the touch of Truth the pent-up forces of the soul are set free. As soon as true love stood at India's door, it flew open; all hesitation and holding back vanished. Truth awakened truth.

Stratagem in politics is a barren policy,—this was a lesson of which we were sorely in need. All honour to the Mahatma who made visible to us the power of Truth. But reliance on tactics is so ingrained in the cowardly and the weak, that in order to eradicate it, the very skin must be sloughed off. Even today, our worldly-wise men cannot get rid of the idea of utilising the Mahatma as a secret and more ingenious move in their political gamble. With their minds corroded by untruth, they cannot understand what an important thing it is that the Mahatma's supreme love should have drawn forth the country's love. The thing that has happened is nothing less than the birth of freedom. It is the gain by the country of itself. In it there is no room for any thought, as to where the Englishman is, or is not. This love is self-expression. It is pure affirmation. It does not argue with negation; it has no need for argument.

Some notes of the music of this wonderful awakening of India by love floated over to me across the seas. It was a great joy to me to think that the call of this festivity of awakening would come to each one of us; and that the true *shakti* of India's spirit, in all its multifarious variety, would at last find expression. This thought came to me because I have always believed that in such a way India would find its freedom. When Lord Buddha voiced forth the truth of compassion for all living creatures, which he had obtained as the fruit of his own self-discipline, the manhood of India was roused and poured itself forth in science and art and wealth of every kind. True, in the matter of political unification the repeated attempts that were then made have often failed; nevertheless India's mind had awakened into freedom from its submergence in sleep, and its overwhelming force would brook no confinement within the petty limits of country. It overflowed across ocean and desert, scattering its wealth of the spirit over every land that it touched. No commercial or military exploiter, today, has ever been able to do anything like it. Whatever land these exploiters have touched has been agonised with sorrow and insult, and the fair face of the world has been scarred and disfigured. Why? Because not greed but love is true. When love gives freedom it does so at the very centre of our life. When greed seeks unfettered power, it is forcefully impatient. We saw this during the partition agitation. We then compelled the poor to make sacrifices, not always out of the inwardness of love, but often by outward pressure. That was because greed is always seeking for a particular result within a definite time. But the fruit which love seeks is not of today or tomorrow, nor for a time only: it is sufficient unto itself.

So, in the expectation of breathing the buoyant breezes of this new found freedom, I came home rejoicing. But what I found in Calcutta when I arrived, depressed me. An oppressive atmosphere seemed to burden the land. Some outside compulsion seemed to be urging one and all to talk in the same strain, to work at the same mill. When I wanted to inquire, to discuss, my well-wishers clapped their hands over my lips, saying: 'Not now, not now'. Today, in the atmosphere of the country, there is a spirit of persecution, which is not that of armed force, but something still more alarming, because it is invisible. I found, further, that those who had their doubts as to the present activities, if they happened to whisper them out, however cautiously, however guardedly, felt some admonishing hand clutching them within. There was a newspaper which one day had the temerity to disapprove, in a feeble way, of the burning of cloth. The very next day the editor was shaken out of his balance by the agitation of his readers. How long would it take for the fire which was burning cloth to reduce his paper to ashes? The sight that met my eye was, on the one hand, people immensely busy; on the other, intensely afraid. What I heard on every side was that reason, and culture as well, must be closured. It was only necessary to cling to an unquestioning obedience. Obedience to whom? To some *mantra*, some unreasoned creed!

And why this obedience? Here again comes that same greed, our spiritual enemy. There dangles before the country the bait of getting a thing of inestimable value, dirt cheap and in double-quick time. It is like the *fakir* with his gold-making trick. With such a lure men cast so readily to the winds their independent judgement and wax so mightily worth with those who will do not do likewise. So easy it to overpower, in the name of outside freedom, the inner freedom of man. The most deplorable part of it is that so many do not even honestly believe in the hope that they swear by. "It will serve to make our countrymen do what is necessary", say they. Evidently, according to them the India which once declared: "In Truth is victory, not in untruth" that India would not have been fit for *Swaraj*.

Another mischief is that the gain, with the promise of which obedience is claimed, is indicated by name, but is not defined. Just as when fear is vague it becomes all the more strong, so the vagueness of the lure makes it all the more tempting; in as much as ample room is left for each one's imagination to shape it to his taste. Moreover, there is no driving it into a corner because it can always shift from one shelter to another. In short, the object of the temptation has been magnified through its indefiniteness while the time and method of its attainment have been made too narrowly definite. When the reason of man has been overcome in this way, he easily consents to give up all legitimate questions and blindly follows the path of obedience. But can we really afford to forget so easily that delusion is at the root of all slavery—that all freedom means freedom from *maya*? What if the bulk of our people have unquestingly accepted the creed that by means of sundry practices *Swaraj* will come to them on a particular date in the near future, and are also ready to use their club to put down all further argument—that is to say, they have surrendered the freedom of their own minds and are prepared to deprive other minds of their freedom likewise,—is not this by itself a reason for profound misgiving? We were seeking the exorcizer to drive out this very ghost; but if the ghost itself comes in the guise of exorcizer, then the danger is only heightened.

The Mahatma has won the heart of India with his love; for that we have all acknowledged his sovereignty. He has given us a vision of the Shakti of truth; for that our gratitude to him is unbounded. We read about truth in books; we talk about it; but it is indeed a red-letter day, when we see it face to face. Rare is the moment, in many a long year, when such good fortune happens. We can make and break Congresses every other day. It is at any time possible for us to stump the country preaching politics in English. But the golden rod which can awaken our country in Truth and Love is not a thing which can be manufactured by the nearest goldsmith. To the wielder of that rod our profound salutation! But having seen truth, our belief in it is not confirmed, what is the good of it all? Our mind must acknowledge the truth of the intellect, just as our heart does the truth of love. No Congress or other outside institution succeeded in touching the heart of India. It was roused only by the touch of love. Having had such a clear vision of this wonderful power of Truth, are we to cease to believe in it, just where the attainment of *Swaraj* is concerned? Has the truth, which was needed in the process of awakenment, to be got rid of in the process of achievement?

Let me give an illustration. I am in search of a *vina* player. I have tried East and I have tried West, but have not found the man of my quest. They are all experts, they can make the strings resound to a degree, they command high prices, but for all their wonderful execution they can strike no chord in my heart. At last I come across one whose very first notes melt away the sense of oppression within. In him is the fire of the *shakti* of joy which can light up all other hearts by its touch. His appeal to me is instant, and I hail him as master. I then want a *vina* made. For this, of course are required all kinds of material and a different kind of science. If, finding me to be lacking in the means, my master should be moved to pity and say: "Never mind, my son, do not go to the expense in workmanship and time which a *vina* will require. Take rather this simple string tightened across a piece of wood and practise on it. In a short time you will find it to be as good as a *vina*". Would that do? I am afraid not. It would, in fact, be a mistaken kindness for the master thus to take pity on my circumstances. Far better if he were to tell me plainly that such things cannot be had cheaply. It is he who should teach me that merely one string will not serve for a true vina; that the materials required are many and various; that the lines of its moulding must be shapely and precise; that if there be anything faulty it will fail to make good music, so that all laws of science and technique of art must be rigorously and intelligently followed. In short, the true function of the master player should be to evoke a response from the depths of our heart, so that we may gain the strength to wait and work till the true end is achieved.

From our master, the Mahatma,—may our devotion to him never grow less!—we must learn the truth of love in all its purity, but the science and art of building up *Swaraj* is a vast subject. Its pathways are difficult to traverse and take time. For this task, aspiration and emotion must be there, but no less must study and thought be there likewise. For it, the economist must think, the mechanic must labour, the educationist and statesman must teach and contrive. In a word, the mind of the country must exert itself in all directions. Above all, the spirit of inquiry throughout the whole country must be kept intact and untrammelled, its mind not made timid or inactive by compulsion, open or secret.

We know from past experience that it is not any and every call to which the country responds. It is because no one has yet been able to unite in *yoga* all the forces of the country in the work of its creation, that so much time has been lost over and over again. And we have been kept waiting and waiting for him who has the right and the power to make the call upon us. In the old forests of India, our *gurus*, in the fulness of their vision of the Truth had sent forth such a call saying: "As the rivers flow on their downward course, as the months flow on to the year, so let all seekers after Truth come from all sides". The initiation into Truth of that day has borne fruit undying to this day, and the voice of its message still rings in the ears of the world.

Why should not our *Guru* of today, who would lead us on the paths of *Karma,* send forth such a call? Why should he not say: "Come ye from all sides and be welcome. Let all the forces of the land be brought into action, for then alone shall the country awake. Freedom is in complete awakening, in full self-expression". God has given the Mahatma the voice that can call, for in him there is the Truth. Why should this not be our long-awaited opportunity?

But this call came to one narrow field alone. To one and all he simply says: "Spin and weave, spin and weave". Is this the call: "Let all seekers after Truth come from all sides?" Is this the call of the New Age to new creation? When nature called to the bee to take refuge in the narrow life of the hive, millions of bees responded to it for the sake of efficiency, and accepted the loss of sex in consequence. But this sacrifice by way of self-atrophy led to the opposite of freedom. Any country, the people of which can agree to become neuters for the sake of some temptation, or command, carries within itself its own prisonhouse. To spin is easily, therefore, for all men it is an imposition hard to bear. The call to the ease of mere efficiency is well enough for the bee. The wealth of power, that is man's, can only become manifest when his utmost is claimed.

Sparta tried to gain strength by narrowing herself down to a particular purpose, but she did not win. Athens sought to attain perfection by opening herself out in all her fulness,—and she did win. Her flag of victroy still flies at the mast-head of man's civilisation. It is admitted that European military camps and factories are stunting man, that their greed is cutting man down to the measure of their own narrow purpose, that for these reasons joylessness darkly lowers over the West. But if man be stunted by big machines, the danger of his being stunted by small machines must not be lost sight of. The *Charkha* in its proper place can do no harm, but will rather do much good. But where, by reason of failure to acknowledge the differences in man's temperament, it is in the wrong place, there thread can only be spun at the cost of a great deal of the mind itself. Mind in no less valuable than cotton thread.

Some are objecting: "We do not propose to curb our minds, for ever, but only for a time". But why should it be even for a time? It is because within a short time spinning will give us *Swaraj*? But where is the argument for this? *Swaraj* is not concerned with our apparel only–it cannot be established on cheap clothing; its foundation is in the mind, which, with its diverse powers and its confidence in those powers, goes on all the time creating *Swaraj* for itself. In no country in the world is the building up of *Swaraj* completed. In some part or other of every nation, some lurking greed or illusion still perpetuates bondage. And the root of such bondage is always within the mind. Where then, I ask again, is the argument, that in our country *Swaraj* can be brought about by everyone engaging for a time in spinning? A mere statement, in lieu of argument, will surely never do. If once we consent to receive fate's oracle from human lips that will add one more to the torments of our slavery and not the least one either. If nothing but oracles will serve to move us, oracles will have to be manufactured, morning, noon and night, for the sake of urgent needs, and all other voices would be defeated. Those for whom authority is needed in place of reason, will invariably accept despotism in place of freedom. It is like cutting at the root of a tree while pouring water on the top. This is not a new thing, I know. We have enough of magic in the country,—magical revelation, magical healing, and all kinds of divine intervention in mundane affairs. That is exactly why I am so anxious to re-instate reasons on its throne. As I have said before, God himself has given the mind sovereignty in the material world. And I say today, that only those will be able to get and keep *Swaraj* in the material world who have realised the dignity of self-reliance and self-mastery in the spiritual world, those whom no temptation, no delusion, can induce to surrender the dignity of intellect into the keeping of others.

Considering the burning of cloth, heaped up before the very eyes of our motherland shivering and ashamed in her nakedness. What is the nature of the call to do this? Is it not another instance of a magical formula? The question of using or refusing cloth of a particular manufacture belongs mainly to economic science. The discussion of the matter by our countrymen should have been in the language of economics. If the country has really come to such a habit of mind that precise thinking has become impossible for it, then our very first fight should be aginst such a fatal habit, to the temporary exclusion of all else if need be. Such a habit would clearly be the original sin from which all our ills are flowing. But far from this, we take the course of confirming ourselves in it by relying on the magical formula that foreign cloth is 'impure'. Thus economics is bundled out and a fictitious moral dictum dragged into its place.

Untruth is impure in any circumstances, not merley because it may cause us material loss, but even when it does not, for it makes our inner nature unclean. This is a moral law and belongs to a higher plane. But if there be anything wrong in wearing a particular kind of cloth, that would be an offence against economics, or hygiene, or aesthetics, but certainly not against morality. Some urge that any mistake which brings sorrow to body or mind is a moral wrong. To which I reply that sorrow follows in the train of every mistake. A mistake in geometry may make a road too long, or a foundation weak, or a bridge dangerous. But mathematical mistakes cannot be cured by moral maxims. If a student makes a mistake in his geometry problem and his exercise book is torn up in consequence, the problem will nevertheless remain unsolved until attacked by geometrical methods. But what if the schoolmaster comes to the conclusion that unless the exercise books are condemned and destroyed, his boys will never realise the folly of their mistakes? If such conclusion be well-founded, then I can only repeat that the reformation of such moral weakness of these particular boys should take precedence over all other lessons, otherwise there is no hope of their becoming men in the future.

The command to burn our foreign clothes has been laid on us. I, for one, am unable to obey it. Firstly, because I conceive it to be my very first duty to put up a valiant fight against this terrible habit of blindly obeying orders, and this fight can never be carried on by our people being driven from one injunction to another. Secondly, I feel that the clothes to be burnt are not mine, but belong to those who most sorely need them. If those who are going naked should have given us the mandate to burn, it would, at least, have been a case of self-immolation and the crime of incendiarism would not lie at our door. But how can we expiate the sin of the forcible destruction of clothes which might have gone to women whose nakedness is actually keeping them prisoners, unable to stir out of the privacy of their homes?

I have said repeatedly and must repeat once more that we cannot afford to lose our mind for the sake of any external gain. Where Mahatma Gandhi has declared war against the tyranny of the machine which is oppressing the whole world, we are all enrolled under his banner. But we must refuse to accept as our ally the illusion-haunted magic-ridden slave-mentality that is at the root of all the poverty and insult under which our country groans. Here is the enemy itself,on whose defeat alone *Swaraj* within and without can come to us.

The time, moreover, has arrived when we must think of one think one, and that is this. The awakening of India is a part of the awakening of the world. The door of the New Age has been flung open at the trumpet blast of a great war. We have read in the *Mahabharata* how the day of self-revelation had to be preceded by a year of retirement. The same has happened in the world today. Nations had attained nearness to each other without being aware of it, that is to say, the outside fact was there, but it has not penetrated into the mind. At the shock of the war, the truth of it stood revealed to mankind. The foundation of modern, that is Western, civilisation was shaken; and it has become evident that the convulsion is neither local nor temporary but has traversed the whole earth and will last until the shocks between man and man, which have extended from continent to continent, can be brought to rest, and a harmony be established.

From now onwards, any nation which takes an isolated view of its own country will run counter to the spirit of the New Age, and know no peace. From now onward, the anxiety that each country has for its own safety must embrace the welfare of the world. For some time the working of the new spirit has occasionally shown itself even in the Government of India, which has had to make attempts to deal with its own problems in the light of the world problems. The war has torn away a veil from before our minds. What is harmful to the world, is harmful to each one of us. This was a maxim which we used to read in books. Now mankind has seen it at work and has understood that wherever there is injustice, even if the external right of possession is there, the true right is wanting. So that it is worthwhile to sacrifice some outward right in order to gain the reality. This immense change, which is coming over the spirit of raising it from the petty to the great, is already at work even in Indian politics. There will doubtless be imperfections and obstacles without number. Self-interest is sure to attack enlightened interest on evey step. Nevertheless it would be wrong to come to the decision that the working of self-interest alone is honest, and the large-hearted striving is hypocritical.

After sixty years of self-experience, I have found that out and out hypocrisy is an almost impossible achievement, so that the pure hypocrite is a rarity indeed. The fact is, that the character of man has always more or less of duality in it. But our logical faculty, the trapdoor of our mind, is unable to admit opposites together. So when we find the good with the bad, the former is promptly rejected as spurious. In the universal movement, as it becomes manifest in different parts of the world, this duality of man's character cannot but show itself. And whenever it does, if we pass judgement from past experience, we are sure to pronounce the selfish part of it to be the real thing; for the spirit of division and exclusion did in fact belong to the past age. But if we come to our judgement in the light of future promise, then shall we understand the enlightened largeheartedness to be the reality, and the counsel which will unite each to each to be the true wisdom.

I have condemned, in unsparing terms, the present form and scope of the League of Nations and the Indian Reform Councils. I, therefore, feel certain that there will be no misunderstanding when I state that even in these, I find signs of the Time Spirit, which is moving the heart of the West. Although the present form is unacceptable, yet there is revealed an aspiration, which is towards the truth, and this aspiration must not be condemned. In this morning of the world's awakening , if in only our own national striving there is no response to its universal aspiration, that will betoken the poverty of our spirit. I do not say for a moment that we should belittle the work immediately to hand. But when the bird is roused by the dawn, all its awakening is not absorbed in its search for food. Its wings respond unwearingly to the call of the sky, its throat pours forth for songs for joy of the new light. Universal humanity has sent us its call today. Let our mind respond in its own language! For response is the only true sign of life. When of old we were immersed in the politics of dependence on others, our cheif business was the compilation of others' shortcomings. Now that we have decided to dissociate our politics from dependence, are we still to establish and maintain it on the same recital of other's sin? That state of mind so engendered will only raise the dust of angry passion, obscuring the greater world from our vision, and urge us more and more to take futile short cuts for the satisfaction of our passions. It is a sorry picture of India, which we shall display if we fail to realise for ourselves the greater India. This picture will have no light. It will have in the foreground only the business side of our aspiration. Mere business talent, however, has never created anything.

In the West, a real anxiety and effort of their higher mind to rise superior to business considerations, is beginning to be seen. I have come across many there whom this desire has imbued with the true spirit of the *Sannyasin*, making them renounce their home-world in order to achieve the unity of man, by destroying the bondage of nationalism; men who have within their own soul realised the *Advaita* of humanity. Many such have I seen in England who have accepted persecution and contumely from their fellow countrymen in their struggles to free other peoples from the oppression of their own country's pride of power. Some of them are amongst us here in India. I have seen *Sannyasins* too in France-Romain Rolland for one, who is an outcast from his own people, I have also seen them in the minor countries of Europe. I have watched the faces of European students all aglow with the hope of a united mankind, prepared manfully to bear all the blows, cheerfully to submit to all the insults, of the present age for the glory of the age to come. And are we alone to be content with telling the beads of negation, harping on others' faults and proceeding with the erection of *Swaraj* on a foundation of quarrelsomeness? Shall it not be our first duty in the dawn to remember Him, who is one, who is without distinction of class or colour, and who with His varied *shakti*, makes true provision for the inherent need of each and every class; and to pray to the Giver of Wisdom to unite us all in right understanding.

6

CHRONOLOGY OF EVENTS

1861 — Rabindranath Tagore born on 7 August, 1861 in Calcutta.

1866 — Started learning the alphabet.

1868 — Admitted to Oriental Seminary and then to Normal School.

1869 — Made his first attempt at versification.

1870 — Studied general science, elementary geometry, arithmetic, geography, history, physiology, anatomy, drawing and music with the help of private tutors at home.

1871 — Admitted to the Bengal Academy

1872 — His first acquaintance with the countryside of Bengal.

1873 — Visited Santiniketan for the first time and composed a drama, *Prithiviraj Parajaya*.

1874 — Prepared a verse—rendering of Macbeth. Admitted to the St. Xavier's School in Calcutta.

1875 — Recited a patriotic poem at the *Hindu Mela*. His mother expired.

1876 — His first literary criticism of a book of Bengali poems appeared in *Jnanankur*. Visited Shelidah for the first time.

1877 — Made his first stage appearance in the principal role in a comedy written by Jyotirindranath.

1878 — Sent to Ahmedabad to study English. He contributed series of articles on English life and letters and also on the romantic love of poets like Dante, Petrarch and Goethe, to *Bharati*. Sailed to England and attended the school at Brighton.

1879 — Admitted to the University College in London and studied English literature. Visited the British Museum frequently. Started writing his first verse-drama, *Bhagnahriday*. Attended a session of the House of Commons.

1880 — Returned to India without completing any course of study. Took part in a private performance of Jyotirindranath's drama, *Manmoji.*

1881 — Composed his first set of devotional songs for the anniversary of Brahmo Samaj. His first musical play staged at the Jorasanko house. His two books, *Rudrachanda* and *Bhagnahriday* were published. Delivered his first public lecture on 'Music and Feeling' with vocal demonstration at Calcutta Medical College. Started writing his first extent novel, *Bauthakuranir Hat.*

1882 — Assisted Jyotirindranath in establishing Sarasvat Samaj. Visited Darjeeling for the first time.

1883 — Started writing the poems of *Chhabi O Gan.* Started contributing series of articles to the monthly *Bharati,* dealing with the futile and merely verbal political agitation of those days. Married Mrinalini Devi on 9 December.

1884 — His sister-in-law, Kadambari Devi passed away. Dedicated three of his books to her memory. Appointed Secretary of the Ali Brahmo Samaj.

1885 — His first essay on Raja Rammohun Roy was brought out as a brochure. Edited an anthology of *Vaishnava* lyrics in collaboration with his friend Srish Chandra Majumdar. The first collection of his serious essays came out as *Alochana.*

1886 — Engaged in controversies over social and socio-religious subjects. His first child, Madhurilata born on 25 October. Received his first literary prize in the form of a handsome cheque from his father on account of the devotional songs composed for the anniversary of the Brahmo Samaj.

1887 — Started composing the *Manasi* group of poems marked by a distinct note of originality and vigour both in theme and technique. Read a paper on Hindu marriage criticizing the system of early marriage. Visited Darjeeling with his family and started writing his musical play, *Mayar Khela.*

1888 — The first collection of his essays in literary criticism on various subjects appeared under the title *Samalochana.* His eldest son, Rathindranath born on 27 November.

1889 — Visited Sholapur. Wrote his first five-act drama, *Raja O Rani* in blank verse.

1890 — Read a paper at a public meeting in Calcutta protesting against the reactionary anti-Indian policy of Lord Cross, the then Secretary of State for India and advocated appointment of elected representatives of the people as members of the Viceroy's Executive Council. Took charge of the management of the Tagore Estates with Shelidah as his headquarters. Sailed for England on 22 August. Visited Italy and France on the way. Returned India on 4 November. Attended the sixth session of the Indian National Congress in Calcutta.

1891 — His second daughter, Renuka born on 23 January. His first crop of six short stories published in the *Bengali Weekly*, *Hitabadi*. Prepared the first draft of his well-known drama in blank verse, *Chitrangada*. Participated in the festivals connected with the consecration of the prayer-hall at Santiniketan.

1892 — Toured frequently in North Bengal. Established good contact with the life of the people. Spent the summer at Santiniketan. Started writing the poems of *Sonar Tari* which punctuated a land-mark in his poetry.

1893 — Visited Cuttack on estate business. Read a paper on *Ingraj O Bharatvasi* at a public meeting with Bankimchandra Chatterji in the chair. Returned Santiniketan to attend the third anniversary of Seventh *Paush*.

1894 — His third daughter, Mira born on 12 January. Read a paper at a memorial meeting held in Calcutta in honour of Bankimchandra Chatterji. Elected Vice-President of the newly founded Bangiya Sahitya Parishad. Took over the editorial charge of *Sadhana*.

1895 — Wrote a series of remarkable short stories beginning with *Kshudita Pashan*. Read a paper on the future of Bengali literature at the anniversary of the foundation of the Sahitya Parishad. Attended the anniversary of Seventh *Paush* at Santiniketan.

1896 — Toured Orissa in connection with the partitioning of the Tagore estates. The first collected edition of his poetical works, *Kavyagranthavali* published. His youngest son, Samindranath born on 12 December.

1897 — Attended the Bengal Provincial Conference at Natore. Felicitated his friend, J.C. Bose on the successful demonstration of some of his experiments before the Royal Society in London.

1898 — Took over the editorial charge of *Bharati*. Read a paper entitled *Kantharodh* at a public meeting in the Town Hall of Calcutta in protest against the Sedition Bill drafted by the Secret Press Committee. Wrote strongly against the reactionary policy of the Government with particular reference to the arrest of Tilak on a charge of writing and publishing seditious articles in *Kesari* alleged to have led to the murder of Mr. Rand, Plague Officer of Bombay. Actively participated in raising funds for Tilak's defence. Attended the Dacca session of the Bengal Provincial Conference and read a summary in Bengali of the Presidential address by Rev. Kalicharan Banerjee delivered in English.

1899 — His family removed to Santiniketan. Helped Sister Nivedita in organising relief for plague victims in Calcutta. Assisted in raising funds for the Bengali poet Hemchandra Banerji who had gone blind.

1900 — Published *Katha* chronicling the deeds of heroism and martyrdom in Rajput, Maratha and Sikh history—all seeking to inspire in the young a spirit of deep patriotism and a pride in the nations's storied past, and *Kahini* based mostly on mythological themes.

1901 — Visited Allahabad. Composed the poems of *Naivedya*, an inspiring exposition in verse of the spiritual values of the Indian way of life. His two daughters, Madhurilata and Renuka got married. Contributed to *Bharati* a humorous play, *Chirakumar Sabha*, completing the last instalment in record time. He was instrumental in getting financial support for J.C. Bose from the Maharaja of Tripura to enable him to complete his work in England. Established a school at Santiniketan on 22 December.

1902 — Faced severe financial difficulties to run the school. Sold his house property at Puri and a part of his personal library. Gave a new interpretation to the history of India in a thought provoking article, *Bharatvarsher Itihas*. Joined in the countryside agitation against Lord Curzon's insinuation of the Eastern characteristic of 'exaggeration or extravagance' and wrote a trenchant retort in *Bangadarsan* quoting instances of England's lying propaganda against the Boers in South Africa. His wife passed away on 23 November.

1903 — His second daughter, Renuka passed away in September. The first proposal for the partition of Bengal published in the *Calcutta Gazette*.

1904 — His growing interest in the political problems of the country found expression in a series of essays culminating with Swadeshi Samaj in which he stressed the need of rural reconstruction based on mutual aid. Visited the scene of Buddha's enlightenment at Bodhgaya. Supported the movement initiated by Tilak for honouring the memory of Sivaji and wrote a poem on him. Started writing several books for school use, including *Ingaraji Sopan* which introduced for the first time the direct method of teaching English to Bengali children.

1905 — His father passed away on 19 January. Translated into Bengali verse the first four chapters of the Buddhist scripture *Dhammapada*. Criticised in an article the proposal of an Education Committee which recommended that text-books for primary schools of Bengal should be written in four regional dialects of Bengal and three of Bihar. Took the editorial charge of a new Bengali monthly *Bhandar* and created in the pages of the new journal a forum for dis- cussion of important current topics. Visited Agartala and read a paper on *Desiya Rajya* appealing to the rulers of the Indian States to patronise indigenous arts and crafts in preference to luxury products of foreign make. Took active interest in the founding of the Indian Art Society. Advocated a policy of constructive non-cooperation in his paper. Lead a huge procession through the streets of Calcutta singing the *Rakhi* song. Came into close contact with the eminent educationist, Satischandra Mukheriji, founder of the Dawn Society of Caluctta. Took active part in formulating proposals for the establishment of a National Council of Education which sought to provide education on national lines to students expelled from Government institutions for political offences.

1906 — Sent Rathindranath to the University of Illinois at Urbana to study Agriculture. Paid tribute to the brave victims of police repression in different parts of the new province of East Bengal. Invited to preside over the first session of *Bangiya Sahitya Sammilani*. Wrote a series of articles on problems of education. Pleaded for unanimous acceptance of Surendranath Banerje as the sole accredited political leader of Bengal seeking to consolidate the discipline of the people in personal allegiance to a single individual.

1907 — Wrote an article, *Byadhi O Pratikar*, advocating a change of heart and acceptance of a radical social programme for the attainment of real and abiding freedom. Severely criticised for his sudden withdrawal from political activities by many of his contemporaries. His youngest daughter, Mira married on 6 June. His major novel, *Gora*, started appearing in *Pravasi* serially. Presided over the adjourned first session of *Bangiya Sahitya Sammilani*. His youngest son, Samindranath, passed away, on 23 November.

1908 — Presided over the annual Bengal Conference at its Patna session on 11 February when the political atmosphere was still surcharged with the excitement following the unhappy split at Surat. Delivered his presidential address in Bengali thus departing for the first time from the prevailing vogue of English, reiterating his call to young men of Bengal to dedicate themselves to constructive work in villages and to the work of bringing Hindus and Muslims together in corporate work, for the well-being of the Bengali community as a whole. Organised village uplift work in the Patisar region of the Tagore estates. Started delivering a series of sermons at Santiniketan Mandir almost day after day for a period of nearly six months. These are later collected in a series of booklets entitled *Santiniketan.* Presided over the opening of the new premises of Bangiya Sahitya Parishad in Calcutta.

1909 — Delivered a sermon entitled *Navajuger Utsav* on the occasion of the anniversary of the Brahmo Samaj. The first anthology of his selected poems appeared under the title *Chayanika*. His son, Rathindranath returned from America. The first English translation of one of his short stories published in the December issue of *The Modern Review.*

1910 — Rathindranath married to Pratima Devi on 29 January. The English translation of his short story, *Hungry Stones* appeared in the February issue of *The Modern Review*. The monthly *Sahitya* published a series of scurrilous articles severely criticising his literary works. Attended the anniversary of 7 *Paush* at Santiniketan and addressed the congregation.

1911 — At the anniversary of the Brahmo Samaj delivered a sermon in Calcutta entitled *Karmayog*. Assumed editorship of *Tattvabodhini Patrika*—an old established Bengali journal devoted to philosophy and religion. Read a paper at a meeting in Calcutta on the proposed Hindu University. Composed his famous song, *Janȧ-gana-mana-adhinayaka* which was sung for the first time at the twenty-sixth session of the Indian National Congress in Calcutta.

1912 — Read a paper at the prayer hall of the Sadharan Brahmo Samaj entitled *Atmaparichay* in which he referred to the element of universalism in the Hindu view of life and deprecated the separatist tendencies of a certain section of 'reformed' Hindus. The Government of East Bengal and Assam issued a confidential circular that the school at Santiniketan was altogether unsuitable for the education of the sons of Government servants. Delivered a lecture at a public meeting in Calcutta on *Bharatvarsha Itihasher Dhara*. Arrived in London on 16 June. Rothensteine arranged on 30 June a reading of his poems at his house before May Sinclair, Ernest Rhys, Robert Travelyan, Ezra Pound, Alice Meynell, Henry Nevison and others. At the Trocadero, he met some of the leading literary men and intellectuals of England of the day. Met Bernard Shaw, H.G. Wells, Stopford Brooke, W.H. Hudson, Sturge Moore, John Galsworthy, Robert Bridges and others. Sailed for the United States of America and reached New York on 28 October. Delivered a series of discourses on metaphysical topics at Unity Club. In November the India Society of London published a limited edition of *Gitanjali*.

1913 — Left Urbana for Chicago. Delivered lectures on the *Ideals of Ancient Civilisation of India* at the University of Chicago and on *The Problem of Evil* at the Unitarian Hall of Chicago. He attended the Congress of Religious Liberals and spoke on Race Conflict. Macmillan and company, London, published a popular edition of *Gitanjali* followed by *The Gardener*, *The Crescent Moon* and *Chitra*. Sailed for England. The Irish Theatre organised a performance of *The Post Office*. Delivered a series of six lectures at the Caxton Hall under the auspices of the Quest Society. Sailed for India on 4 September. The authorities of the University of Calcutta resolved to confer on him the honorary degree of D.Litt. On 26 December at a special Convocation the University of Calcutta conferred the degree of D.Litt. on him. Andrews paid his first visit to Santiniketan.

1914 — At a special reception at Government House, the Governor, Lord Carmichael, formally handed over the Nobel Prize Diploma and Medal to him on behalf of the Swedish Academy. His book of poems, *Ustraga*, dedicated to Andrews. Regularly contributed essays, stories, and poems to *Sabujpatra*. Delivered a remarkable sermon at Santiniketan entitled *Ma Ma Himsi* on 5 August. A group of students and teachers of Phoenix Settlement came to reside at Santiniketan on an invitation extended by Tagore at the instance of Andrews. Addressed the congregation at Santiniketan Mandir on the occasion of the anniversary of Seventh *Paush* and Christmas.

1915 — Delivered a remarkable address at the inauguration of *Bangiya Hitasadhan Mandali* on *Karmayajna*. Read the completed play before the staff and students at Santiniketan. The first visit by a high government official took place on 20 March when Lord Carmichael, the Governor of Bengal, came to Santiniketan. Left for a fortnight's holiday in Kashmir. Read a paper at a public meeting in Calcutta on *Sikshar Bahan* urging the adoption of the mother tongue alongside of English as the medium of instruction in the Universities of India.

1916 — Advised village workers to introduce systematic tree-planting. Accepted invitation from the Pond Lyceum to undertake a lecture-tour of the United States of America. Delivered his first lecture in Japan at the Imperial University, Tokyo. His two lectures on 'The Nation' and 'The Spirit of Japan' in which he condemned the spirit of aggressive nationalism latent in Japan's imperialist policy towards China, roused considerable resentment. Received an invitation from Canada to visit Vancouver on his way to the States. On 7 September sailed for Seattle, U.S.A. His first lecture engagement took place in the hall of the Sunset Club. Sailed for Japan from San Francisco on 21 January 1917.

1917 — Reached Japan at the end of January. After one month stay in Japan, returned to Calcutta. On 4 August read at a public meeting in Calcutta his famous political paper *Kartar Ichchhay Karma.* Supported the candidature of Annie Besant for the Presidentship of the Indian National Congress Session in Calcutta, against the opposition of the 'moderate' group. The communal riot in Bihar provoked from his pen a scathing analysis of the bureaucratic system of government in his paper *Chhoto O Baro*. Returned to Santiniketan and received Sir Michael Sadler and other members of the Calcutta University Commission. Placed his views on education before the Commission, the members of which were deeply impressed by his educational experiment at Santiniketan.

1918 — Started writing a series of story-poems later published as *Palataka*. His eldest daughter, Madhurilata passed away on 16 May. Wrote books for class use for coordinated teaching of English and Bengali. Formulated his idea about creating an institution which would be a true centre for the different cultures of the East, and the foundation stone of Visva-Bharati laid with proper ceremony.

1919 — Delivered a public lecture at the Empire Theatre on 27 March on the Centre of Indian Culture in Calcutta. Started a new monthly, *Santiniketan Patra*. The nucleus of Visva-Bharati formed on 3 July. Gandhi invited him to attend a Gujarati Literary Conference in Ahmedabad. Tagore took the residence in a mud-cottage.

1920 — On 2 April presided over the Gujarati Literary Conference at Ahmedabad. Visited Bhavnagar, Limbdi, Nadiad. Decided to go to the West in order to speak about Visva-Bharati and raise funds for it. Stayed for a few days at Petersfield as guest of Murihead Bone. Visited Bristol at the invitation of Professor Lenard. In London, he met the well-known Irish leader Horace Plunkett. Left England on 6 August for France. Met Le Brun, Sylvain Levi, Bergson and other writers and scholars of France with whom he discussed his idea of Visva-Bharati as a centre of inter-cultural understanding. Left France and proceeded to Rotterdam on 19 September. Addressed meetings at Amsterdam, Rotterdam, the Hague and Utrecht. Moved over to Belgium. His lecture took place in the Palace of Justice. Resolved to go to America for they must listen to the appeal of the East and sailed for New York. His first lecture took place on 10 November at Brooklyn.

1921 — Delivered lecture at Harvard University on 25 January. At a farewell meeting organised by the Poetry Society of New York he was not able to repress his feeling of frustration. Proceeded to Chicago on 1 February. Reached London on 24 March. Spoke on "The Meeting of the East and the West", at a meeting of Indian students on 8 April. His first trip by air took place on 16 April. Pearson returned to Santiniketan on 26 September. Started writing the poems on *Sisu Bholanath* series.

1922 — Completed writing his drama, *Muktadhara*. Warned his countrymen against the spirit of violence vitiating the Non-cooperation Movement. On 6 February the Rural Reconstruction Institute at Santiniketan was formally inaugurated with Elmhirst as its first Director. Visva-Bharati started a Local Committee in Calcutta. Addressed the students of the Presidency College on 21 August on the ideals of Visva-Bharati. Delivered a series of lectures at Colombo and Galle. In Bombay discussed the possibility of initiating Zoroastrian studies at Visva-Bharati with the leaders of the Parsi community.

1923 — His second brother, Satyendranath passed away on 9 January. Lord Lytton, Governor of Bengal visited Santiniketan. *Visva-Bharati Quarterly* started publication under his editorship from April. Delivered a lecture on Bankem Chandra at a meeting of Bhowanipore Literary Society on 28 June. Discussed the programme of the newly formed Swaraj Party, and also Hindu-Muslim relations which he said could be strengthened only through the fusion of the economic interests of the two communities.

Pearson passed away in a train accident in Italy on 24 September.

1924 — Attended the anniversary of the Rural Reconstruction Institute at Santiniketan on 6 February. Visited Calcutta and paid his tribute to the poet Manmohan Ghose at a memorial meeting in Presidency College. Delivered a course of three lectures on literature at the University of Calcutta. Sailed for China on 21 March. Received a great ovation enroute at Rangoon, Penang, *Kualampur*, Singapore, Hongkong. Reached Shanghai on 12 April. Addressed a meeting of students at Hangchow on 16 April. Arrived in Peking on 23 April. Returned to India on 21 July. Sailed from Colombo on 24 September. On 18 October Sailed for Argentina. Met the President of the Argentine Republic, Dr. Alvaer, on 30 December.

1925 — Reached India on 17 February. His elder brother, Jyotirindranath passed away on 4 March. Gandhi visited him on 29 May to discuss the ethics of *Khadi*. Tagore publicly criticised for staying out of the *Charkha* campaign. He replied in an article giving his reasons for rejecting *Charkha* as a means of attaining *Swaraj*. C.R. Das passed away on 16 June.

1926 — Attended the All-India Music Conference at Lucknow. His eldest brother, Dwijendranath passed away on 18 January. Delivered lectures at the University of Dacca. Returned to Calcutta in early March. Sailed for Naples on 30 May. Proceeded to Rome and met Mussolini on 31 May. Delivered his first public lecture at the Quirinal Theatre on 'The Meaning of Art', on 8 June.Reached Vienna on 10 July. Sailed for Oslo on 21 August. Addressed the Oriental Academy on 25 August. Met several distinguished Norwegians. Proceed to Germany. Arrived in Berlin on 11 September. From Berlin proceeded to Prague and delivered a few lectures. Reached Belgrade on 15 November. Sailed from Alexandria for India and on board the ship started writing a series of letters to Nirmalkumari Mahalanobis. Returned to Santiniketan on 19 December.

1927 — Presided over the anniversary meeting at Santiniketan advocating a total approach to village problems. Introduced the Nataraja conception of cosmology in a number of poems and songs, suited for interpretation in rhythmic movement and dramatic expression. Left on 28 March for Bharatpur on the Maharaja's invitation to preside over the Hindi Literary Conference. Returned to Santiniketan on 11 April. Sailed from Madras on a tour of some of the South-East Asian countries on 12 July. Delivered so many lectures at several places. Returned to Calcutta on 27 October.

1928 — Attended a meeting in his Calcutta residence at Jorasanko and tried to reconcile differences between two sections of Bengali literary men over the issue of ultra-modernism in literature. Started writing the novel *Sesher Kavita*. Introduced two seasonal festivals, *Vriksharopana* at Santiniketan and *Halakarshana* at Sriniketan. Read a paper on the Message of Rammohan Roy at the centenary celebrations of the Brahmo Samaj in Calcutta on 22 August. Assumed full administrative responsibility for all the institutions at Santiniketan on 10 September. Devoted much time to his new medium of creative self-expression, painting. Lord Irwin, Viceroy of India, visited him at Santiniketan on 17 December.

1929 — Presided over the conference of the International Religions convened on the occasion of the centennial of the Brahmo Samaj on 27 January. Delivered a speech on the Principles of co-operation and pointed out how their application might bring about an all-round improvement of socio-economic life in India. Reached Victoria on 6 April and delivered his lecture on 'The Philosophy of Leisure'. Spoke on 'The Principles of Literature' at Vancouver on 8 April. Left Canada for United States of America in response to an invitation from the Universities of California, Detroit, Harvard, Columbia and Washington. Reached Yokohama on 10 May. On 15 May delivered lectures at a meeting of the Indo-Japanese Association of Tokyo on Oriental Culture and Japanese Mission. Sailed for Indo-China on 7 June. The French Government of Indo-China and the people accorded him a most cordial welcome at a reception given by the Mayor of Saigon. Reached Madras on 3 July. Participated in *Vriksharopama* ceremony at

Santiniketan on 10 August and in *Halakarshana* ceremony at Sriniketan on 11 August. Composed a poem to mark the inauguration on 16 September of the Indian College of the University of Montpellier in France. Takagaki, a well-known exponent of the Japanese Judo joined Santiniketan to teach his art to the students in November.

1930 — Delivered lectures at Baroda on 'Man the Artist' on 27 January and on 30 January discussed problems of education at the Teachers Training College. Arrived in London on 11 May and then proceeded to the Quaker Settlement at Woodbroke near Birmingham. Received news about Salt *Satyagraha* in India. Delivered the Hibbert lectures at Oxford University. Addressed the annual meeting of the Quakers in London on 24 May. Reached Berlin on 11 July and met the members of the Reichstag. Met Einstein on 14 July. Visited Peter Maniche's International People's College at Elsinore on 7 August. Participated in a meeting of the New Education Fellowship at Elsinore. On 15 September visited the Federation of the Union of Cinematographic Artists. Delivered his farewell speech at a big reception organised in the Central House of Trade Unions on 24 September. Sailed for the United States of America on 3 October. The Discussion Guild and the Indian Society of America held a reception at the Carnegic Hall and he spoke on educational problems. Left the United States of America on 18 December and reached England on 23 December.

1931 — Reached Calcutta on 31 January. On 11 May a large gathering of representative citizens of Calcutta met at the Calcutta University Institute Hall and decided to celebrate his seventieth birthday in a grand and fitting manner. Visited Bhopal on 17 July. Communal riots broke out in a number of places in Bengal. On 20 September the *Pandits* of the Sanskrit College in Calcutta conferred on him the title *Kavi-Sarvabhauma*. Paid tribute to Gandhi in an address given at Santiniketan on Gandhi's birthday. Sent the tribute of a poem on the Buddha on the occasion of the opening of the new *Vihara* at Saranath on 20 October. Returned to Calcutta on 23 December to attend the Rabindra-Jayanti. The Jayanti week started on 25

December with the opening of an exhibition illustrating the significant events and activities of his varied life, and a fair.

1932 — Delivered an address at the anniversary of Sriniketan where he said that the human factor was by far the most important in any scheme of national uplift. A group of 'Friends' of the Quaker Society visited him at Santiniketan. Left for Persia on 11 April. Delivered several lectures. Returned to Calcutta on 3 June. Accepted the invitation of the University of Calcultta to take the University Chair of Bengali and also to deliver the Kamala Lectures. Advised his countrymen to get rid of irrational communal and class differences. Received Pandit Madan Mohan Malaviya at Santiniketan on 2 December. Presided over the Seventieth Birthday Anniversary Celebration of Sir P.C. Ray and dedicated to him the brochure *Mahatmaji and Depressed Humanity*.

1933 — Delivered series of three lectures at Calcutta University on the subject of *Manusher Dharma*. Attended the anniversary of Sriniketan of 5 February. Presided over the inaugural meeting of the Rammohan Centenary at Senate Hall, Calcutta on 18 February and delivered an address in English on Rammohan Roy. On 13 April issued a press-statement from Santiniketan emphasising the need of establishing fully equipped information centres in the West. Organised the work of compiling a glossary of technical terms in Bengal. On 12 December addressed a public meeting at Secunderabad on the Ideals of an Eastern University. On 29 December delivered his address *Bharatpathik* Rammohan Roy at the Senate Hall on the occasion of the death centenary of Rammohan.

1934 — Received Sarojini Naidu at Santiniketan on 5 January. Received Jawaharlal Nehru and his wife at Santiniketan on 19 January. On 6 February attended the anniversary of Sriniketan. Presided over the Silver Jubilee of the Hindusthan Co-operative Insurance Company. Sailed for Ceylon on 5 May along with a party of teachers and students of Santiniketan for a cultural tour of Ceylon. Returned to Santiniketan of 28 June and initiated some administrative changes in the institution. Received Khan

Abdul Gaffar Khan at Santiniketan on 31 August. Attended the anniversary of Santiniketan on 23 December.

1935 — Sir John Anderson, Governor of Bengal, visited Santiniketan on 6 February. The Banaras University conferred on him the degree of D.Litt. Addressed the Punjab Students' Fifth Annual Conference on 15 and 17 February. Met leaders of the Sikh Community and visited the *Gurdwara*. Returned to Santiniketan on 4 March. The Journal, *Visva-Bharati Quarterly*, which had ceased publication after 1931, re-appeared in its new series under the editorship of Krishna Kripalani. Wrote a poem on Ramakrishna by way of tribute on the occasion of his centenary.

1936 — Reached Delhi on 25 March and laid the foundation of the prayer hall of the Modern School. Visited Calcutta to preside over a mass meeting held in the Town Hall on 15 July to protest against the discriminatory provisions of the Communal Award. The University of Dacca conferred on him on 29 July the degree of D.Litt.

1937 — Delivered the Convocation Address of the Calcutta University on 17 February. On 3 March addressed the Ramakrishna Centenary Parliament of Religions in Calcutta, on the subject 'Religion of the Spirit and Sectarianism'. Sir John Russel visited Santiniketan and Sriniketan on 8 March. On 2 August addressed a public meeting in the town Hall of Calcutta on the situation created by the hunger-strike of political prisoners in the Andamans. Jagadischandra Bose passed away on 23 November. Wrote a number of poems with an undertone of mystic realisation, during his convalescence, later published as *Prantik*. On 1 March the Osmania University conferred on him the degree of D. Litt. Attended the performance in Calcutta of the dance-drama *Chandalika* presented by the staff and students of Santiniketan on 19 March. Received Dr. Radhakrishnan at Santiniketan on 4 September. Addressed the congregation at the Anniversary of Seventh *Paush* on 23 December.

1939 — Subhaschandra Bose visited Santiniketan on 21 January. Jawaharlal Nehru performed the opening of *Hindu-Bhavana* on 31 January. On 19 August, at the invitation of Subhaschandra Bose laid the foundation-stone of the Mahajati Sadam in Calcutta. The first volume of the *visva-Bharati* edition of his complete works appeared in September.

1940 — On the occasion of the anniversary of the Brahmo Samaj addressed the prayer-hall congregation at Santiniketan on *Purner Sadhana* on 25 January. Attended the anniversary of Sriniketan on 6 February. Gandhi and his wife visited Santiniketan on 17 February. C.F. Andrews passed away on 5 April. On 7 August the Oxford University held a special convocation at Santiniketan to confer on him the degree of D. Litt.

1941 — Addressed at the prayer-hall on the occasion of the anniversary of the Brahmo Samaj on Rammohan on 24 January. On 13 May the Maharaja of Tripura sent a special emissary to confer on him the title of *Bharat-Bhashkar*. Passed away on 7 August.

BIBLIOGRAPHY

Works of Rabindranath Tagore

Gitanjali, The Indian Society, London, 1912.
Sadhana, Macmillan, London, 1913.
Crescent Moon, Macmillan, London, 1913
Stray Birds, Macmillan, London, 1916.
My Reminiscences, Macmillan, London, 1917.
The Cycle of Spring, Macmillan, London, 1917.
Nationalism, Macmillan, London, 1917.
Personality, Macmillan, London, 1917.
The Home and the World, Macmillan, London, 1919.
Greater India, S. Ganesan, Madras, 1921.
Glimpses of Bengal, Macmillan, London, 1921.
Creative Unity, Macmillan, London, 1922.
Letters from Abroad, S. Ganesan, Madras, 1924.
Talks in China, Visva-Bharati, Calcutta, 1925.
Broken Ties and Other Stories, Macmillan, London, 1925.
Letters to a Friend, Allen and Unwin, London, 1928.
Sheaves, Indian Press, Allahabad, 1929.
The Religion of Man, George Allen and Unwin, London, 1931.
Lectures and Addresses, Macmillan, London, 1928.
Selections from Tagore, Macmillan, Indian edition, 1946.
A Vision of Indian History, Visva-Bharati, Calcutta, 1962.
The Religion of an Artist, Visva-Bharati, Calcutta, 1963.
Mahatma Gandhi, Visva-Bharati, Calcutta, 1963.
A Crisis in Civilisation, Visva-Bharati, Calcutta, 1941.

Anthologies and Collected Works

Stories from Tagore, Macmillan, Calcutta, 1918.
Poems from Tagore, Macmillan, Calcutta, 1922.
Lectures and Addresses by Tagore, Macmillan, London, 1928.
Collected Poems and Plays of Tagore, Macmillan, London, 1936.
Towards Universal Man, Asia Publishing House, Bombay, 1961.

Works by Other Authors

Ahluwalia, B.K., *Tagore and Gandhi*, Pankaj Publications, New Delhi, 1981.

Bali, D.R., *Modern Indian Thought*, Sterling Publishers Private Limited, New Delhi, 1984.

Das, T.N., *Rabindarnath Tagore: His Religious, Social and Political Ideals*, Saraswati Library, Calcutta, 1932.

Ghose, S., *Modern Indian Political Thought*, Allied Publishers Private Limited, New Delhi, 1984.

Kripalani, K., *Rabindranath, A Biography*, Oxford University Press, London, 1962.

Radhakrishnan, S., *The Philosophy of Rabindranath Tagore*, Macmillan, London, 1918.

Rabindranath Tagore, *A Centenary Volume*, Sahitya Akademi, New Delhi, 1961.

Roy, N., *An Artist in Life*, University of Kerala, Trivandrum, 1967.

Sen, S., *The Political Thought of Tagore*, General Printers and Publishers, Calcutta, 1947.

INDEX

Abanindranath Tagore, 41
Acharya Brajendra Nath Seal, 45
Acharya Prafulla Chandra Ray, 45, 58
Advaita, 56
Africa, 27
Agitation, 11, 78
Agreement, 34
Agriculture, 60
Ahimsa, 29
Aladdin's lamp, 74, 75
All-India Deshabandhu Memorial, 58
Amar Jagat, 18
Amrita Bazar Patrika, 12
Ananda, 68
Annie Besant, 95
Anti-British propaganda, 36
Ascesticism, 65
Ashram, 20, 40
Atmabodh, 18

Banaphul, 12
Bangadeshan, 71
Bankruptcy, 65, 73
Bengal Academy, 12
Bengal,
  anti-partition movement, 31
  partition of, 11, 38
Bharat Thirtha, 22
Bharati, 13
Brahma, 54
Brahmacharya, 40
Brahacharya Ashrama, 13
Brahmavidya, 68
Brahmin, 23
Brahma Samaj, 24
Buddha, 63

Calcutta University, 14, 23
Chandalika, 24
Charkha, 45, 48, 51, 52, 54, 55, 56, 87, 59, 60, 61, 82
  agitation, 47
Chatterjee, Bankim Chandra, 11
China, 34
Competition, 28, 52, 59
Criticism, 24, 58, 59
Cultural exchanges, 42
Customs, 23

Decentralisation, 26
Deenabandhu, 17
Demoralisation, 43, 63
Despotism, 29
Dharma, 21
Dignity of Labour, 49
Disagreement, 58
Divinity, 52
Dukha, 68
Dutt, Sitanath, 12
Dwija, 50

Economic exploitation, 27
Economic resources, 49
Economic science, 49
Education, 36, 39, 40, 43
  aims of, 39-40
Educational philosophy, 39
Educational system, 40, 41, 42
European civilisation, 29
Events, chronology of, 84-102
Exploitation, 25, 29, 47, 53, 60, 67

Fakir, 79
Food problem, 55
France-Romain Rolland, 86
Freedom, 31
Fruit gathering, 20

Gayatri, 12
Gita, 16, 17, 21
Gitanjali, 14, 19
Gopees, 51
Gurudev, 17
Gurus, 81
Gyanankur, 12

Himsa, 65
Hindu-Muslim conflict, 38
Hindu-Muslim problems, 37
Hindu-Muslim Unity, 36-44, 48
Hinduism, 22
Humanity, 18, 19, 64-66
glorious tradition of, 70
Humanistic interpretation, 25
Humanism, 15-17

Imperialism, 29
Indian National Congress, 14, 28
Indian Reform Council, 85
Infinite, 20, 21
Intermarriage, 38
International organisation, 34

Jagannath Ghat, 45
Jalianwala Bagh, 11, 27
Jana Gana Mana, 13
Japan, 59
war, 34
Japanese imperialism, 33
Jealousy, 58
Jivan Devata, 20
Jhanankur, 87

Kabir, 16
Karma, 46
Karmayoga, 21
Khadi, 45
Khaddar, 52
Khilafat movement, 37
Kshatriya, 23
clan, 17

Lakshmi, 51
League of Nations, 53, 85
Liberal education, 41
London, 93
London University, 13
Lord Buddha, 15, 78
Lord Curzons, 90
Lord Hardinge, 66
Lord Maculay, 42

Machiavellian-State-Craft, 29
Magical revolution, 82
Mahabharata, 84
Maharishi, 12
Mahatma Gandhi, 17, 57, 66, 77, 84
Manchester, 59
Manifestation, 53
Mantra, 79
Mantram, 47
Maya, 66, 71, 74, 76, 79
Milton, 62
Mind, 47
Modern civilisation, 23
Modern Review, 63, 69
Moore, C.A., 19
Mrinalini Devi, 13
Mukti, 24, 68
Mukut for Balak, 13
Muslim Community, 36

National Antham, 13
National Council of Education, 42
National Egoism, 64
National Fund, 14
Nationalism, 27, 32, 33, 34
Negroes, 33
Nirvana, 68
Nobel Prize, 14
diploma, 94
Non-Cooperation,
bustle of, 67
movement, 63-65
religious doctrine of, 69

Occupation, 30, 60, 61
Organisation, 28, 29, 30, 74

Padma, 50
Pakistan, 38
Paris, 59
Partition agitation, 78
Pasteur's law, 56, 57
Patriotism, 33, 52, 69
Political asceticism, 64
Political blackmail, 34
Political programme, 26
Political revolution, 31, 75
Poverty, 38, 43, 50, 51, 53, 57

Professional politicians, 27
Propaganda, 57
Purification, 56

Radhakrishnan, S., 17
Rajrishi, 13
Rajaram Mohan Roy, 12, 32, 57, 62
Raksha-Bandhan,
  ceremony, 38
  festival, 14
Rural education, 32
Russia, 34

Sacrifice, 24
Sadition Bill, 90
Sadhana, 71
Sannyasin, 86
Sarasvat Samaj, 88
Sati, 23
Schiller, F.C.S., 15
Self-aggrandisement, 53
Self-discipline, 78
Self-determination, 70, 73
Self-realisation, 36
Shakespeare, 62
Shakti, 46, 50, 57, 78, 86
Shankara, 60
Shantiniketan, 40, 41
Shastras, 45, 47, 71
Shudras, 24, 50
Sir Horace Plankett, 54, 55
Sita, 59
Soloman, 59
Spiritual Freedom, 25, 64
Spiritual world, 41-42
St. Xavier School, 12
Superstitions, 20
Swadeshi, 31
  agitation, 77
  movement, 27, 65
  Samaj, 72
Swaraj, 31, 49, 51, 52, 54, 55, 56, 64, 69, 71, 79, 80, 81, 82, 83, 84, 86

Tagore's,
  administration of Buddhist Philosophy, 16
  arguments, 61
  basic apprehension, 39
  criticism, 58
  discrimination, 23
  letters, 65
  letter to Gandhji, 62
  message, 30
  nationalism, 33
  political thought, 39
  political views, 25
  social problems, 14
  views on *charkha,* 45-56
  views on Hindu-Muslim unity, 36-44
  voluminous writings, 16
  writings, 13, 31

Universal huminity, 86
Untouchability, 24, 56
Upanishads, 12, 15-16, 36, 54, 69

Varna System, 23
Varnashrama, 23
Vina, 80
Violence, 31, 67
Vishnu, 50, 51
Voluntary Cooperation, 67

Yoga, 35, 75, 81
Young India, 58, 59
The Young Queens Market, 13